Save the Belknap

By

Robert Carney Powers

Copyright © 2011

All rights reserved. No part of this publication may be reproduced, stored in a retrieval system or transmitted in any form or by any means electronic, mechanical, photocopying, recording or otherwise, without the prior written permission of the publisher.

This is a true story.

Published by:
Powerful Publisher LLC
2400 Sterling Point Drive
Virginia Beach, Virginia 23703

Library of Congress and catalog Number:
2011914965

International Standard Book Number (ISBN)
9780982062050

Printed in the United States of America
1ˢᵗ Printing

Dedicated to:

My wife
Phyllis Garris Powers

and to

Shipmates

Prologue

This is not a history. It's a true story as I remember it. The dialogue is a reconstruction intended to represent what was occurring. It is not verbatim dialogue. The analysis of the collision is based on facts documented in the Chief of Naval Operations Investigation (noted in the bibliography).

The officers, chief petty officers and crew of USS CLAUDE V. RICKETTS (DDG-5) were all heroes the night USS JOHN F. KENNEDY (CV-67) AND USS BELKNAP (CG-26) collided. Thanks to them for their service and heroism. They will never be forgotten.

A special thanks to my two Executive Officers, Captain Dave Ricketts (Lieutenant Commander at the time) and Rear Admiral Phil Coady (Lieutenant Commander at the time), both now deceased. Their dedication and top notch performance took me and the ship through many tight passages.

My thanks to the officers of CLAUDE V. RICKETTS who contributed their recollections: Rear Admiral Steve Smith (Lieutenant Commander at the time), Captain Bill Doud (Lieutenant at the time), Captain Garry Holmstrom (Lieutenant at the time), Captain Ben Welch (Lieutenant at the time), Captain Tim Freihofer (Ensign at the time) and Commander Rich Celotto (Ensign at the time). All officers and crew would have gladly assisted, I know. These are the ones with whom I was in touch at the time of the writing.

Thanks to Rear Admiral Milt Schultz (Captain at the time), the squadron commander embarked on my ship on the night of the rescue operations. His support was essential to my success. As I concentrated on my ship and the task at hand, he made decisions that affected the entire force and coordinated the search and rescue operations. His input was essential to the writing of this book.

Thanks to Petty Officer First Class Dennis Eaves, ship's photographer, who took most of the pictures herein. Also, thanks to Mister Peter Ill whose senior paper at

Princeton on the collision and rescue operations provided structure for my memory.

I have included explanations of Navy terms and procedures for readers who may not be familiar with them. So, you old sea dogs, please bear with me.

It is my hope that through reading this account, future generations will be encouraged to choose an adventurous life at sea in service to their country, and that they will avoid the mistakes that led to the collision described herein.

My fondest thanks go to all my shipmates and colleagues in a long Navy career. There's no one closer than a shipmate who has shared the best and toughest of times.

Robert Carney Powers
Captain, U.S. Navy (Retired)
2011

Table of Contents

Chapter		Page
1	The Towering Inferno	9
2	Proceed to Assist	25
3	Getting Ready	27
4	Overhaul	41
5	Guantanamo Bay	79
6	The Mediterranean Sea	97
7	First Approach	115
8	Second Approach	125
9	Third Approach	131
10	Aftermath	147
11	The Investigation	157
12	On Kennedy's Bridge	163
13	On Belknap's Bridge	171
14	Kennedy, After the Collision	181
15	Belknap After the Collision	185
16	The Long Voyage Home	191
17	Analysis of the Collision	203
Epilogue		213
Admiral Claude V. Ricketts		225
The Ship, USS Claude V. Ricketts		227

Table of Contents (Continued)

	Page
U.S.S. CLAUDE V. RICKETTS (DDG-5)	
Officers	229
Chief Petty Officers	230
Commander, Destroyer Squadron TWENTY-TWO (Embarked)	
Officers	231
Chief Petty Officers	231
Schedule, January 1975 – January 1976	233
Awards	237
In Memoriam	241
Bibliography	243

Chapter One
The Towering Inferno

Time Magazine, December 8, 1977
Headline: There It Was
   Driving easily through a moderate sea, the vast U.S.S. John F. Kennedy catapulted jet aircraft into the night about 70 miles east of Sicily. One after another, the F-14 fighters braced on the catapults, revved their engines to a screech, then were flung off the bow of the 87,000-ton carrier. The red glow of their afterburners traced their progress as they climbed into the blackness.
   When all the flight was safely aloft, the 1,047-ft. Kennedy got ready to position herself for the landing operation — "to seek the wind," in the Navy's phrase. All was well. There was nothing difficult about the maneuver; it had been performed thousands of times by units of the U.S. Sixth Fleet in the Mediterranean. The job of the six much smaller ships shepherding the Kennedy was to change position to accommodate the movements of the attack carrier. The Kennedy radioed her planned change of course to the U.S.S. Belknap, a 7,930-ton guided-missile cruiser that was some 3,000 yards off the carrier's port bow. (Author's note: Belknap was actually about 4,000 yards on the carrier's port quarter) The Belknap began a starboard turn (Author's Note; In fact, Belknap slowed and later began a slow turn to port).
   At 10 p.m. taps sounded over the loudspeaker system aboard the Kennedy, and the chaplain went on the ship's closed-circuit TV network to give the evening benediction. The atmosphere was equally relaxed aboard the Belknap.
   Then in an instant, everything changed. Over the Belknap's loudspeaker crackled a call given only if the ship is in peril or coming under attack: "Captain to the bridge!" Gangways (Author's Note: a better term would be passageways) aboard the Belknap filled with jostling men racing to their stations. Fifteen long seconds passed while the men tensed against the unknown (Author's Note. It was actually several minutes between the call for the Captain

and the collision). Then a heavy shock passed through the cruiser, followed by a long, rumbling shudder that felt like an earthquake. Up above, the Kennedy's angled landing deck was smashing through the superstructure of the Belknap like a battering ram. The impact crushed the ship's funnels, sending clouds of acrid smoke billowing through the cruiser. Jet fuel from the Kennedy sluiced over the Belknap's superstructure. Fire broke out on both ships.

USS JOHN F. KENNEDY (CV-67)
Aircraft Carrier, Underway, Before the Collision
(World Wide Web Source)

*****

The ship I commanded, USS CLAUDE V. RICKETTS (DDG-5) was in a screening station approximately sixty-five hundred yards north of the aircraft carrier JOHN F. KENNEDY (CV-67).

USS CLAUDE V. RICKETTS (DDG-5)
Guided Missile Destroyer, Underway
(World Wide Web Source)

There were five ships in a circular screen around KENNEDY patrolling assigned sectors while the carrier conducted flight operations (launching and recovering aircraft). Commander Destroyer Squadron TWENTY-TWO (my Boss), Captain (Commodore) Milton J. Schultz, was embarked in my ship and was in command of all the ships in the screen (A Captain in command of a squadron has the honorary title of Commodore).

At 2145 (that's 9:45 PM for those not familiar with Navy timekeeping). I was in Combat Information Center (CIC) behind my bridge going over a just completed exercise in junior officer maneuver training.

The ships in the circular screen in addition to

RICKETTS were; a LEAHY class cruiser, USS DALE (CG-19), Captain Leland H. Sebring Commanding; a GEARING class destroyer USS BORDELON (DD-881), Commander George E. Pierce, Commanding; a KNOX class frigate, USS PHARRIS (FF-1094), Commander Bruce A. Friedsam, Commanding; and a KNOX class frigate, USS THOMAS C. HART (FF-1092), commanded by a friend from the Naval Academy, Class of 1958, Commander John D. Rorbough. (Note: the Commanding Officer of a commissioned ship of the U.S. Navy is accorded the honorary title of "Captain", no matter his rank.)

The aircraft carrier USS JOHN F. KENNEDY (CV-67) was commanded by Captain William A. Gureck. USS BELKNAP (CG-26) was commanded by Captain Walter R. Shafer.

PHARRIS had earlier been assigned to plane guard duty for KENNEDY. A plane guard ship takes station 1500-4000 yards just to port of the carrier's wake. From this position, the ship is immediately available for rescue operations should an aircraft crash and go into the water. The plane guard ship also serves as a visual reference for the pilot in his landing on the carrier. This is particularly helpful at night. RICKETTS was frequently assigned plane guard duty, as were the destroyer and the frigates.

At about 1845, the Commanding Officer of KENNEDY, assumed tactical command of USS BELKNAP (CG-26) to take the place of PHARRIS as plane guard. The primary reason given for this was that KENNEDY's TACAN (tactical air navigation; a beacon used by aircraft to locate the carrier) was inoperable. BELKNAP had a TACAN that was operable, and could fill in as an aircraft beacon as well as perform plane guard duties.

The formation was on course 200, about 70 miles east of of Sicily. Speed was 10 knots. KENNEDY had launched her aircraft and was preparing to recover them.

BELKNAP was assigned a station on a relative bearing of port 160 degrees from KENNEDY at a range of 4000 yards. This means, in layman's terms, that BELKNAP was just to port (left) of KENNEDY's wake, two nautical miles behind.

Two miles away is not very far when you're dealing with ships of 7,000+ and 87,000+ tons at sea. At that distance, an aircraft carrier looks enormous. And the shape of an aircraft carrier is all boxes and angles that are confusing to the untrained eye. At night, it becomes worse.

USS BELKNAP (CG-26), Before the Collision
(World Wide Web Source)

In CIC, I heard KENNEDY send out the signal "Execute to follow, CORPEN JULIET 025-12". Translated, this meant that the main body (KENNEDY and BELKNAP) would turn left and come to a course of 025 (a 175 degree turn, or almost an "about face") and change speed to 12 knots. The screening ships around the carrier would adjust to the new course as directed by the screen commander (Commodore Schultz).

The carrier was "seeking the wind" to obtain the maximum wind over the deck to recover aircraft (more lift, more control for the pilots). At 2146, the signal was executed (which means, "do it").

At about 2151 (9:51 PM), Lieutenant Junior Grade John Woodhouse, the CIC Officer, advised me that the plots of KENNEDY and BELKNAP showed them coming dangerously close to each other. It looked like the plots would "merge". The Commodore was informed.

I heard KENNEDY ask BELKNAP over PRITAC

(Primary Tactical Maneuvering Radio Circuit), "What are your intentions?"

For a seaman, these words send a chill up your spine. It means that two ships are in close proximity and neither one understands what the other is doing. It means that there is imminent danger of collision. There's an old Navy saying "a collision at sea can ruin your whole day."

As I ran from CIC to the bridge, collisions of years past flashed through my mind. I had read about them all and nearly experienced one myself.

*****

One such collision occurred between the FORREST SHERMAN class destroyer U.S.S. EDWARDS (DD-950) and the ESSEX class aircraft carrier U.S.S. BENNINGTON (CVS-20) off the coast of California on 11 August 1960. The carrier was damaged slightly. The port side of the destroyer's superstructure was crushed. The collision was attributed steering loss by EDWARDS.

By far the most dangerous condition is when warships are maneuvering in close proximity either in battle or training, as were BELKNAP and KENNEDY.

On 11 March 1956, the 13,600-ton BALTIMORE class heavy cruiser U.S.S. COLUMBUS (CA-74) collided with the 2,425 ton GEARING class destroyer U.S.S. FLOYD B. PARKS (DD-884). The cruiser sheared off the bow of the destroyer just forward of its number one five inch gun mount during night time task group maneuvering operations. Two men were killed. It would have been worse had not PARKS been at General Quarters (GQ) with the highest watertight integrity set (all major hatches secured) and the crew out of the forward berthing areas (primarily Chief's Quarters).

The light aircraft carrier H.M.A.S. MELBOURNE (R21) of the Royal Australian Navy (RAN) and the ALLEN M. SUMNER class destroyer U.S.S. FRANK E. EVANS (DD-754) of the United States Navy collided on 3 June 1969. The two ships were participating in exercises in the South China Sea. EVANS steamed under

MELBOURNE'S bow and was cut in two. Seventy-four of her crew were lost. The collision was attributed to negligence by officers of EVANS.

On a night in 1963 (can't recall the exact date), I was the Officer of the Deck (OOD) aboard the ALLEN M. SUMNER class destroyer U.S.S. LAFFEY (DD-724). We were steaming with U.S.S. RANDOLPH (CVS-15) in waters east of Virginia conducting anti-submarine warfare exercises. It was night and the carrier was running fast.

Destroyers were in a screen around her. The order came over PRITAC to reorient the screen to an axis corresponding to an upcoming carrier change of course. As usual, I could "see" the relative motion picture in my head. I changed course and added speed to take my ship toward her new station. The turn was executed.

CIC called out a calculated course to station which was close to the one I had "seen". I walked out to the starboard wing of the bridge and looked back at the carrier. All I could see was a blob of red lights, making it very difficult to determine which part of the big ship I was seeing.

Immediately, I didn't like what I saw. The red blob was getting bigger and its bearing was not changing. As the blob got closer, I could see that I was looking at her port bow just aft of my starboard beam. She had not yet turned to starboard to her new course! Instinctively I reacted.

"All engines ahead flank, make turns for twenty seven knots," I ordered. "Left full rudder."

I remained on the starboard wing of the bridge and watched my ship gradually pull away from the carrier. Then, she disappeared past my stern.

I ran to the port bridge wing. I saw a starboard bow aspect on the carrier. I shifted the rudder and matched the carrier's course. I had caught it in time. I was a little weak kneed as I thought about all of the men who were depending on me to keep their ship out of trouble.

Commander Mel Rogers (Commanding Officer, USS LAFFEY) came to the bridge just in time for the Admiral to come up on PRITAC and indicate his displeasure. Fortunately, the Captain absorbed the ass chewing and let me live to conn (control the ship) another day. I am forever thankful to Captain Rogers for having confidence in me. He was a great Captain. A real "steamer" as the Navy saying goes.

*****

I reached the bridge of RICKETTS hoping that in the few seconds it took me to get there, KENNEDY and BELKNAP would extricate themselves from their difficulty and all would be well.

TIME Magazine: Aboard the Belknap, an explosion blew Machinist's Mate Michael F. Cartolano Jr., 20, through a hatch into a bulkhead. He staggered on deck and looked up in horror. "The Kennedy was sitting right on top of us with her deck on fire," he recalls. "There it was — a nightmare!"

RICKETTS Sailors stare at the towering inferno that was BELKNAP
(Photograph by Dennis Eaves)

From RICKETTS, some three miles away from BELKNAP, I saw a sheet of flame leap into the sky. It silhouetted BELKNAP as she passed down the port side of KENNEDY. A billowing fireball rose into the sky.

I could see BELKNAP drift astern of KENNEDY. Both ships were on fire. I remember cringing. It's was as though I felt the pain of the men on BELKNAP that were crushed and burned. It was as if I was on BELKNAP's bridge and felt the pain in my heart that I knew was crushing Captain Shafer. Every Captain values his crew more than his ship, and his ship is his life. I remember feeling physically sick for a moment.

My years of training kicked in. I turned to Lieutenant Garry Holmstrom, my Officer of the Deck (OOD). "Set the rescue and assistance detail. We're going in".

TIME Magazine: On a nearby destroyer, the U.S.S. Claude V. Ricketts, the loudspeaker ordered: "Away the rescue and assistance team!" As the Ricketts prepared for action, her stunned Sailors witnessed an awesome sight. "You know that movie, Towering Inferno?" Yeoman Roshon King, 20, later asked. "That's what the Belknap looked like."

"This is the Captain, I have the conn." I announced it for all to hear.

Things were a little shaky. I knew the crew needed to hear the voice of someone in charge; someone who knew what to do. Inside, I wasn't yet sure I did. But for them, I was sure. I knew I'd figure it out.

"Right full rudder. All engines ahead full." I heard my orders as if detached, watching some horror flick.

I headed my ship for the flaming BELKNAP.

I was calm, yet a bit frightened. My training and experience had steeled me to deal with threatening situations, yet I knew that there were many dangerous variables in the equation for success in this one. This wasn't Vietnam, but it looked to be very close to a combat situation. All of the things that my ship would have to do flashed through my mind. I disciplined myself to focus on the most important thing for me; conn the ship and do my best to minimize the danger to ship and crew. The crew was well trained and I had superior officers. They would have to take care of the rest.

BELKNAP Burns and Explodes as RICKETTS
Approaches
(Photograph by Dennis Eaves)

*****

Milt Schultz paced the pilot house as I raced out to the starboard bridge wing. A thousand things ran through his mind as he geared up to face what he could see was dangerous, unknown, and had the potential for intense personal hazard.

Milt grew up on a wheat farm in Kansas where he was the only farm hand for his grandfather's farm at harvest. He drove a tractor, learned machinery, milked cows, drove mules and gardened. He delivered papers in all kinds of weather. He entered the Navy as an enlisted man and was trained as a hospital corpsman before obtaining an appointment to the Naval Academy. He attended the Naval Preparatory School (NAPS) in Bainbridge, Maryland and graduated from the Academy with the Class of 1950. He had commanded ships, seen and accomplished much. This night would be a mighty test of his experience and capability.

Milt knew it was wise to use RICKETTS to close BELKNAP, as she was best equipped to save the situation. Using DALE (a large cruiser) was a risk of valuable force structure. The size of RICKETTS was a better fit alongside BELKNAP.

He knew RICKETTS Sailors had set high standards in the ship yard, and the machinery aboard his flagship was reliable. Critical to the rescue operation were the ship's six main fire pumps. It was going to be a long night of pumping water. RICKETTS had the potential needed to fight the conflagration. He also wanted to be close to the action to better enable his decision making.

Milt felt a shiver of concern, a brief fear of the unknown. Then, his years at sea and training came into play. He knew what was expected of him. He just had to think of everything that had to be done, and quickly!

"Captain, what are your intentions," asked Milt.

"I'm going to go in there, put the whaleboat in the water and see if anyone went overboard, Sir."

"Okay. I'm going to designate you as the primary fire fighting ship. Get your ship ready."

"Aye aye, Sir."

I turned to the OOD. "Set General Quarters, Garry."

"Aye aye, Captain." Garry was a blonde headed officer with a baby face who could drop and give you a hundred pushups in a minute or so. I knew I could depend on him.

Lieutenant Commander Phil Coady, my Executive Officer showed up on the bridge. As usual, he stood beside me sizing up the situation. Phil was a Boston Irishman with a terrific sense of humor who knew not only what to do, but how to back me up.

"I've got the Chiefs on deck organizing hose teams," said Phil.

I could hear the excitement in his voice, though it was

controlled excitement. As usual, Phil and I were thinking the same way. I was preoccupied with conning the ship. He was a step ahead of me in organizing the ship to do what had to be done. There were many things to do. With an Exec like Phil, I knew they would be done without my having to issue an order.

On the main deck, the hose teams and damage control parties were getting organized. Every Chief Petty Officer who did not have a general quarters station critical to the task at hand was on deck providing leadership; Master Chief Fire Control Technician (Missiles) Austin, Master Chief Fire Control Techincian (Missiles) Hooper, Chief Electronics Technician Barker, and Chief Fire Control Technician (Guns) Bonin,

*****

Ensign Rich Celotto, the Main Propulsion Assistant, was in charge below decks in Main Engine Control. Rich was a quietly competent young officer with engineering "know how". He was standing Engineering Officer of the Watch (EOOW) with Machinist Mate First Class Parker as Top Watch, and Machinist Mate Fireman Redfoot as Throttleman.

Redfoot stood in front of the large wheel on the throttle board. Gauges showed the number of turns (revolutions per minute the shaft was making), the steam pressure and other essential information. The nearby engine order telegraph (EOT) dial indicated the latest order from the bridge for the engines.

The main turbines hummed as they drove one of RICKETTS' two main shafts that turned the screws. It was almost times for "taps" and the engine room was stinky hot as usual.

Over the 1MC (ship's announcing system), "Away the rescue and assistance detail."

"Sounds like the Bo'sun piped the wrong call," mused Rich.

Then, soon after came the words, "General Quarters! General Quarters! This is not a drill. All hands man your battle stations!"

The Main Control crew looked at each other with concern. Something serious was happening. Down in the bowels of the ship, anything "serious" was doubly so. Deep in the ship with tons of heavy, fast moving machinery and hundreds of pipes laden with 1200 psi (pounds per square inch) steam that could burst and scald, any emergency was life threatening. In the after engine room, Chief Machinist Mate McKinney readied his crew for the challenges he could feel were coming.

The EOT rang up maneuvering bells (set up for ship maneuvers rather than steady speed), then ahead full (twenty knots). The rudder angle indicator went to full right. Redfoot spun the throttle open, pouring more 1200 psi superheated steam into the turbine. He fought to get the speed of his shaft up as the ship leaned into the turn. (In a tight turn, one shaft wants to slow down, so it takes a lot of steam to keep its speed up, or in this case, crank it up more.)

"I wonder if we're trying to dodge a torpedo," exclaimed Parker as he watched the steam pressure fall and fight to go back up. In the nearby Boiler Room, Ensign Ralph McGee, Boiler Officer, Chief Boiler Techincian Hunt and their Sailors were increasing fuel and feed water to the boiler to send more energy to the turbines.

"I heard there was a Russian ship shadowing us," said Rich. "Something's sure going on!"

Sailors began pouring down the ladder into Main Control. An Electrician's Mate Third Class called Eggplant (a real skinny kid) slid down the ladder in his skivvies carrying his dungarees. He pulled them on as he made his way to his station at the Forward Switchboard as the EOT rang up all ahead flank (a step above full speed).

Lieutenant Commander Steve Smith came down the ladder to Main Control as the ship righted itself after the turn and gathered speed. Steve was the Chief Engineer (CHENG, as he was called), a big good looking guy with a smooth way about him. When the wardroom officers were up to some mischief, which could be depended on, Steve was usually at the center of it.

"What's happening, Cheng," asked Rich, wide eyed.

"Collision," said Steve. "I think BELKNAP ran into the carrier. Anyway, she's on fire."

"Where're we going?" asked Parker.

"Headed for BELKNAP. How many fire pumps are on line?"

"Two," answered Rich.

"Get all six going. And raise the pressure up to about 150 psi (normally around 100 psi). I got a feeling we're gonna need 'em.

"Aye aye, Sir."

Steve examined the gauges on the main control board. "Everything holding?"

"Yes Sir."

"Tell the fire rooms to bring all four boilers on line. I want 'em on quickly, but I don't want to burn anything up."

"I got it," said Rich.

Master Chief Electrician's Mate Linn was busy at the ship's main electrical switchboard. Loss of power in any part of the ship during the rescue operations would critically limit the capability to repond. He was going to make sure that didn't occur.

About that time, the 1MC announced "The ship is proceeding to assist USS BELKNAP. BELKNAP is on fire."

Master Chief Groce slid down the ladder to main control to join Rich. He knew every inch of the engine room and all the machinery in it. The engines were going to be put to the test that night, and he knew it. He wasn't about to let any part of the engineering plant cause a problem. He knew I had enough problems to deal with already.

Steve went back up the long ladder to the main deck interior passageway. As the ship rolled in the seas and vibrated from the thrust of the big engines, he climbed up two decks to the pilot house. He needed to "get the big picture".

The ship was approaching the flaming BELKNAP as

Steve entered the pilot house. Steve saw that I had the conn. There was a silence, a tension in the pilot house that said it all. The ship was standing into danger.

Steve saw Phil.

"XO, I'm bringing all boilers and fire pumps on line," said Steve.

"Okay, I'll tell the Skipper. Get Damage Control Central organized. I think we're going alongside to fight the fires."

"Right."

Steve watched for a few moments, saw the magnitude of what we were dealing with, and went down to Damage Control (DC) Central. In DC Central, Lieutenant Junior Grade Greg Geist, the Damage Control Assistant (DCA), waited for tasking. Greg was a very intelligent officer with a sly grin, as if he always knew something you didn't. He usually did.

Intense Fires Burn Aboard BELKNAP, Midships Starboard Side
(Photograph by Dennis Eaves)

"The action's going to be on the main deck," said Steve. "Send the three repair parties (a team of Sailors trained and organized to fight any damage to the ship) topside, tell' em to prepare to fight the fire on BELKNAP from alongside."

Greg got on the sound powered phones and issued the orders. "Where's the most action?" he asked.

"Probably on the foc'sle," answered Steve. Foc'sle is short for "forecastle", the main deck on the bow of the ship.

"I'll take Repair 2 to the foc'sle," said Greg. He was out the hatch and on his way.

Steve went to the ASROC (anti-submarine rocket) deck amidships and took charge of Repair 5. He sent Repair 3 to the fantail (the main deck at the stern of the ship). He coordinated the efforts of the two repair parties.

Lieutenant Junior Grade Rob McDonough, Fire Control Officer ("fire control" in Navy terminology means control of the the aiming of missiles and guns), ran to assist the repair parties as did Chief Warant Officer Ed Loboda, Electronics Material Officer. On a destroyer, all major evolutions are "all hands" efforts.

Hull Technician First Class Randolph McClary, the Sailor with the most damage control experience, moved about to all three Repair Parties and helped set up to fight the fires. McClary was a muscular, compact black Sailor who had always displayed considerable leadership capability. He was immediately "in charge".

*****

Lieutenant Bill Doud, the Operations Officer, a gruff talking, hard partying, highly competent, all Navy kind of guy, was sitting with the XO in his stateroom discussing implementation of a new training program when "away the rescue and assistance detail" was sounded on the 1MC. He knew immediately that this was unusual at sea. It meant an aircraft crash or collision. He and Phil were on their feet and out the door when the GQ alarm sounded.

Bill grabbed his "Incident Reporting" instruction and headed for CIC. He knew it would be his job to make the necessary reports to higher authority. Phil and Bill raced topside. BELKNAP was a flaming torch, visible for miles around. They made their way to CIC.

"XO, can I write the OPREPS (operation reports) and send 'em out?" asked Bill. "You and the Captain are going to be busy."

"By all means," said Phil. "Do it."

Bill pulled out a message form and started writing, "both ships are afloat and afire"...

Phil told me that he had authorized Bill to release the messages. I concurred, knowing that I would be busy with conning the ship and Phil would be needed on deck coordinating all of the necessary actions.

We sent the initial OPREP-3 PINNACLE report (a required report for a major emergency) and something like 19 SITREPs (situation reports). Bill was busy, assited by John Woodhouse and Ensign Mike Nemechek, the Elecrtonic Warfare Officer. One of those reports declared a "BENT SPEAR" emergency. BELKNAP's magazines were designed to carry nuclear tipped anti-air and anti-submarine weapons.

After the first PINNACLE went, the radiomen set-up a full period termination with the Naval Communications Station Nea Makri in Greece and were pumping them out with great efficiency.

*****

On the bridge, I conned from the starboard wing and watched BELKNAP and her fires grow from a distant horror to an up close tragedy. KENNEDY was pulling away from BELKNAP, her port angled flight deck on fire.

The bridge was absolutely quiet except for the whine of the ship's forced draft blowers (that forced air down to the fires in the boilers) and the sound of the bow cutting through the dark waters. There was no panic, just a sense of professionalism. Garry, the OOD, was calm and in control. Ensign John Pic, the ASW Officer, was the JOOD. Both were officers who had my full confidence.

None of us knew what the next hours would bring, but there was no hesitation.

BELKNAP's Starboard Side Midships, Ablaze With Fires
After the Collision
(You can see the outline of the ship's boats)
(Photograph by Dennis Eaves)

Navy men were in danger. Some might be in the water. Others horribly burned. We knew our duty.

*****

Chapter Two
Proceed to Assist

At about 2220, COMMANDER TASK FORCE SIXTY (CTF 60) assigned COMDESRON TWENTY-TWO duty as the on-scene commander for search and rescue (SAR).

At about 2227, as RICKETTS charged toward BELKNAP, CTF 60 sent a message that said, in effect, "assisting ships should not hazard their vessels."

Milt was informed of the message. His reaction, "How could he do the task and not assume some risk." He dutifully passed the message along to the ships under his command.

No one informed me of the message, as I had the conn and was fast approaching a very hazardous situation. Not that it made much difference. We had to do what we had to do.

*****

Lieutenant Ben Welch, my Supply Corps Officer, called "The Pork Chop" (after the Supply Corps insignia that, to some, resembled a pork chop) was a medium sized guy with a big heart and bigger muscles. At the Naval Academy, he had been a wrestling champion. If the officers didn't agree with his budget, he'd arm wrestle them to decide the issue, and he always won.

Ben was in the wardroom when the call came over the 1MC for General Quarters. He went immediately to a hatch, looked out and saw BELKNAP on fire with a flame roughly three to four times the height of her superstructure shooting up from her stack. To him, it looked like a butane lighter turned up, like some kid might do.

Ben ran to his GQ station in CIC. He found out we were looking for possible men in the water and went up to the signal bridge to help.

When he arrived on the signal bridge, he was greeted by the Sailors there. They had the "Big Eyes" (a large pair of pedestal mounted binoculars) focused on the surrounding waters. Nearby, the flames aboard BELKNAP were so hot they began to melt her aluminum superstructure.

BELKNAP's Boat Davits on the Starboard Side Midships Collapse Amid a Shower of Sparks as the Aluminum Superstructure Melts
(Photograph by Dennis Eaves)

*****

I could see men huddled on the stern of BELKNAP. There were a few men on the cruiser's foc'sle. Amidships, she was ablaze. She was drifting, having lost all power.

Amidships on BELKNAP were three inch gun mounts (port and starboard), chaff rocket launchers (CHAFFROC), pyrotechnic and ready service ammunition lockers for the three inch fifty caliber guns, and triple torpedo tubes (port and starboard) for Mark 46 anti-submarine torpedoes. These were all immersed in fire.

Forward of the bridge was a missile launcher and below that the missile magazine. A thought flashed through my mind; that forward missile magazine was nuclear capable. I didn't know whether there were nuclear weapons there or not. If there were, and fires got to that magazine, there could be an explosion that hurled radioactive material all over BELKNAP and RICKETTS. A nuclear detonation was extremely unlikely. The weapons were built in a way to prevent that occurrence.

On the after end of BELKNAP was a five inch gun mount. Below that, a magazine filled with gunpowder and projectiles. The fires were, at that time, amidships on BELKNAP. We had to do everything we could do to keep the fires away from those ammunition magazines fore and aft. We had to deal with the ammunition amidships as fast as we could. We had our own ammunition to worry about. Lieutenant Junior Grade Al Creasy, Gunnery Assistant, Master Chief Gunner's Mate Roney and Senior Chief Gunner's Mate Manning kept a constant check to be sure our magazines wee not being damaged.

The cruiser had collided with KENNEDY'S port side and passed under the overhang of her angled flight deck. The flight deck had sheared off everything above BELKNAP'S bridge and toppled her two stacks. The collision had burst aviation fuel pipes under KENNEDY'S flight deck overhang. The volatile fuel saturated the midships section of BELKNAP, went down her stacks and was ignited by the cruiser's boiler fires,

BELKNAP's boiler fires were extinguished by the initial explosions. Captain Shafer ordered all engineering spaces to be evacuated as heavy black smoke from burning aviation fuel engulfed them.

At about 2238, my ship was close enough to BELKNAP that if there were men in the water, we should find them.

I ordered "search for men in the water."

*****

Boatswain's Mate Third Class Affonso greeted Ben on the signal bridge. He was of Portuguese descent, famous among shipmates for the chourico (sausage) sent by his mother from Rhode Island. Rotund and cheerful, he was ready for anything.

Sparks Rain Down on RICKETTS' Signal Bridge (One Deck Above the Bridge) as Fires Burn and Shells Explode on BELKNAP
(Photograph by Dennis Eaves)

Phil was below on the bridge. He looked up, saw Ben and Affonso. "Ben, we're going to need fenders—lots of 'em," shouted Phil.

Ben didn't need any coaching. "Come on, Boats," he said as he latched on to Affonso. "We're the fender detail."

Ben and Affonso descended to the main deck and broke out fenders, large and small, including gigantic "bull fenders" used when ships moored alongside one another. Ben and Boats lowered the fenders to the foc'sle and hauled them to position on the starboard side (the side engaged with BELKNAP).

At about 2238, RICKETTS was close enough to BELKNAP that her fire hoses could reach the fire. Twelve fire hoses began to shower the fire using 150 psi pressure from RICKETTS' six fire pumps.

Ben looked down at the foc'sle GQ team. They were huddled forward of the five inch gun mount, directing their hoses at the fires. Burning material showered down on them. Chief Boatswain's Mate Jerry Pugh and Chief Storekeeper Carlos Soltes were in charge.

As RICKETTS came within hose distance, Steve directed the hose teams amidships to keep a hose on the torpedo tubes, as these contained the most explosives.

The three inch ammunition, pyrotechnics and CHAFRROC began to "cook off" (explode due to being heated by the fire.) The night was illuminated as rounds shot up into the air.

Some of the Sailors on the foc'sle bolted when the rounds started going off. Sparks showered down on them Chief Soltes never stopped playing water on the fire. Chief Pugh went after the Sailors. But he didn't have to.

Ensign Tim Freihofer, the Disbursing Officer, was coming through the port break just below the bridge. Tim was a well put together athlete, small in stature, but big in heart and muscle. He motioned to the Sailors "get back up there." They were more afraid of Tim than the fire, so they turned around. Tim led them back to their hose.

*****

When the ship went to general quarters Tim was in the wardroom along with several other officers watching a movie. On the GQ call they immediately made their way out onto the weather deck near the port break to check out what was going on. The fire on BELKNAP was impressive, almost overwhelming. At a distance of a couple miles it looked to be 1000 feet into the sky.

The ship was turning hard to starboard, gathering speed amid 6-12 foot swells, a light rain and bone chilling cold. I was on the starboard wing of the bridge. I watched the curl of the bow wave as we gathered speed and turned. Even at that distance, the white of the wave caught the glow of the fires on BELKNAP. Below decks, the crew was responding, rushing to break out damage control equipment and man fire hoses. The ship was vibrating with the throb of its big turbines and the spirit of the men I was taking toward--who knew at that time?

*****

Tim made his way to his GQ station in radio central as the Crypto Officer (Coding Officer). Upon arriving in Radio Central, he found Bill Doud setting up to write and transmit reports. Bill gave Chief Radioman Gerald Hale and Tim specific direction as to what was expected. Chief Hale mobilized the radiomen to be sure we had optimum communications and could "get the word out."

At about midnight, DESRON TWENTY-TWO Chief Staff Officer, Lieutenant Commander Gerry Lewis arrived in radio and took a rather large chunk of Tim and Chief Hale's butt, saying that all the outgoing messages should originate from COMDESRON TWENTY-TWO, not RICKETTS.

Bill came into radio central as this was going on and refereed. He solved the issue by adding a short sentence at the end of the next SITREP stating this and all preceding SITREPS should be originated from COMDESRON TWENTY-TWO. This placated Gerry and allowed the messages to continue unabated.

Bill also sent a message that said essentially "all reports should be viewed as originated by COMDESRON TWENTY-TWO."

Bill got chewed out by the Commodore for this, but he absorbed the ass chewing and did a magnificent job of "getting the word out." I didn't find out about all this until after the incident. The Commodore never brought it up with me, so we all "got over it." This was a small occurrence compared to the magnitude of the event. The DESRON staff and my officers worked well together.

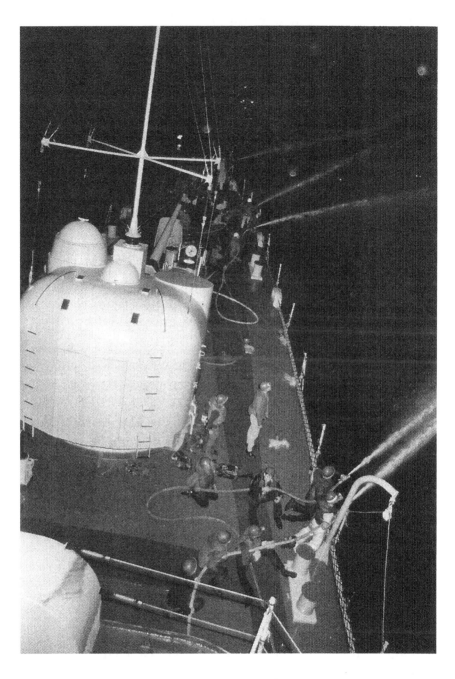

A View From RICKETTS' Bridge of the Fire Hose Teams
on the Ship's Forecastle as She Approaches BELKNAP
(Photograph by Dennis Eaves)

Later, the Commodore told me, "the beauty of the whole operation was the degree of cooperation and synergism between the ship's CIC and Staff of COMDESRON TWENTY-TWO in handling the flow of demand for our help. He also told me much later that "the Naval War College used our crisis management and information flow to higher authority as the model on how to do it, what detail is required, and the excellent results which our reporting engendered."

*****

Gerry Lewis was in his cabin when he heard the GQ alarm sound. He rushed to CIC. Almost immediately, the Commodore ordered him to assemble the staff.

Gerry (later Captain) was a steady hand for Commodore Schultz. He was thorough, knew what the Commodore wanted, checked on the details and saw that the big decisions got to him. He worked well with Phil Coady. He later became a Destroyer Squadron Commander himself.

Lieutenant Bill Slover, the Squadron Material Officer, was an experienced engineer. In this emergency, he became the coordinator for all the ships for damage control equipment that needed to be passed to BELKNAP.

Lieutenant Chuck Hoffman, the Squadron Operations Officer was a calm and authoritative voice for the Commodore on the tactical radio circuits. The circuits were active that night as reports and requests for assistance flew back and forth over the air waves.

Many things had to happen quickly. After a brief discussion, Milt issued his orders;

At 2208-(10:18 PM), we shifted to clear (uncoded) call signs to facilitate timely exchange. BORDELON was stationed upwind of BELKNAP. She would fight the fire as best she could from that position. She did that competently and bravely.

At 2118, Dale was ordered to take station to stern of Belknap and downwind for medical evacuation as needed. HART took station 1500 yards astern of BELKNAP, prepared to provide assistance on whatever came up. PHARRIS was assigned to assist KENNEDY extinguish fires. She approached KENNEDY, but was unable to get close enough to be effective due to the overhang of the carrier's flight deck (where the fires were).

Passive sonar condition was set to protect personnel that might be in the water (active sonar sends out a strong acoustic PING that at close range can be damaging to personnel in the water).

DALE was designated as medical evacuation ship. DALE had a helicopter deck and could receive helicopters from KENNEDY to pick up the wounded and return them to KENNEDY (once her flight deck was again operable). From there, they could be flown to a hospital in Italy. The problem was getting the wounded to DALE.

All ships were ordered to put boats in the water to search for possible men overboard and to remove wounded from BELKNAP. All ships were also directed to set up emergency trauma centers to treat the worse cases and stabilize them for further transportation to DALE.

At 2227, helicopters from KENNEDY were available but couldn't be used over BELKNAP'S burning hull due to the flames. They were used only for medical evacuation of seriously injured personnel on to KENNEDY from DALE and outlying destroyers and frigates.

*****

By 2215, BELKNAP was dead in the water ahead of me a few hundred yards away. I slowed the ship, and backed full until I had bare steerageway.

"Stand by to launch the motor whaleboat."

Garry responded, "Aye aye, Sir."

I turned slightly to provide a lee for the launching of the whaleboat. Back at the port boat davits, Lieutenant Junior Grade Alan Kraft (First Lieutenant and Boat Officer) and Coxswain Boatswain's Mate Second Class Newton Price climbed aboard the motor whaleboat with a boat engineer and two seamen.

"Whaleboat manned and ready, Captain."

"Lower away," I responded. I looked over the side at the tossing seas. It was going to be a rough ride in the twenty-six foot, diesel powered motor whaleboat. Soon the whaleboat was away from the ship, bobbing up and down in six to eight foot swells, searching for men in the water. The Boatswain's Mate of the Watch (BMOW) on the bridge had a hand held radio used to communicate with the whaleboat.

Soon, Al Kraft reported that no personnel had been found in the water. I could see that there were wounded personnel on the fantail of BELKNAP.

"Tell the whaleboat to go to BELKNAP'S stern and remove any wounded personnel."

*****

In the whaleboat, Al and Newton faced a formidable task. As they approached BELKNAP, they could see the ocean swells rising and falling at the stern.

Newton put the whaleboat up against the stern. A seaman threw a line to BELKNAP. One second they were at deck edge, the next they were six to eight feet below the deck. Up and down, and then up and down again.

Men on BELKNAP had to time it. When the whaleboat was at deck edge, they passed a wounded man over to the seaman in the whaleboat as Newton adjusted the engine and spun the wheel to keep the boat steady for a few precious seconds.

RICKETTS' whaleboat took on several wounded men and pulled away from BELKNAP's stern. They returned to RICKETTS, were hoisted to deck edge and the wounded men taken aboard.

I maneuvered the ship at slow speed to recover the whaleboat. Milt ordered his staff doctor, Dr. Roger Leiberman, to go to DALE and set up a Trauma unit.

Roger was an ophthalmologist by training and had never had to deal with burn and crush injuries. His was a terrific challenge. He reported to the whaleboat to be taken to DALE.

Survivors Grouped on the Fantail of BELKNAP Awaiting Whaleboat Rescue.
(Photograph by Dennis Eaves)

Ben was grabbed by the junior hospital corpsman, Petty Officer Second Class Wilson. "Chief Coleman needs you in the wardroom!"

Ben headed with him to the wardroom, where Chief Hospital Corpsman Jim Coleman was setting up for emergency surgery.

Ben's first aid training was primarily received in the Boy Scouts. Jim, of course, had years of training, but was not a Doctor. He had qualified for "independent duty" which in Navy lingo means he could serve as the senior medical person aboard a ship that was not assigned a doctor.

In destroyers, one doctor is normally assigned to a destroyer squadron staff (as was Doctor Leiberman). An independent duty hospital corpsman (essentially a "physician's assistant") is assigned to each ship. Chief Coleman was assisted by Hospital Corpsman Second Class Wilson and Chief Yeoman Bowman in setting up the emergency trauma center in the wardroom.

Doctor Lieutenant Roger Leiberman as RICKETTS'
Whaleboat is Lowered.
(Photograph by Dennis Eaves)

Soon the first burn victim arrived. He had received second, third and fourth degree burns and suffered from smoke inhalation. He was in shock.

They made sure the man's breathing was unobstructed

and administered morphine. Jim showed Ben how to administer morphine; push the plunger in before giving the shot in the thigh to release the drug. They cleaned the wounds, removed dead tissue and applied an antibiotic ointment. Sterile gauze dressings were applied. Plentiful water was given to the burned men to offset loss of fluids.

The RICKETTS team worked frantically as more wounded arrived. Some had broken or crushed limbs which had to be temporarily stabilized. The goal was to stabilize the wounded men, relieve pain and get them ready for transfer to DALE, on to KENNEDY, and then to a hospital in Italy.

The Doctor was embarked in the boat, and once again, it was lowered into the rolling seas.

I'm sure nothing in medical school prepared Roger for that whaleboat ride, or for what he would face aboard DALE. Soon, dozens of burned and injured men would be under his direct care. This would be a night far from the usual physicals, pills for a cold or caring for Sailors after a hard night's liberty. A far cry from every day "sick call".

*****

At 2245, the Commodore ordered me to take RICKETTS closer to BELKNAP, alongside if necessary.

"All engines ahead one third."

RICKETTS approached Belknap. More ammunition cooked off. BELKNAP's starboard boat davits collapsed in a shower of smoke and sparks. Fire hoses showered the burning ship with water. Hoses on the signal bridge were used to douse the canvas flag bags as sparks showered the ship.

I remembered the Commodore's words, "Get your ship ready."

*****

Chapter Three
Getting Ready

"Getting ready" to save the Belknap really began when I was growing up in Portsmouth, Virginia. Portsmouth is a Navy town and I was the son of a naval officer. Dad (Rear Admiral Robert Davis Powers, Jr.) was a Navy Lawyer. At the time, Navy lawyers were line officers with a legal code designator. Today, they wear staff corps insignia and are members of the Judge Advocate General (JAG) Corps.

Dad is considered the "father" of the JAG Corps, being a strong advocate and architect of its creation. He was a lawyer, but first and above all, he was a line officer and "pure Navy."

During the Cuban Missile Crisis of 1962, Dad was assigned to the International Law Division, Office of the Judge Advocate General of the Navy. When President Kennedy wanted to blockade Cuba to prevent the arrival of Soviet land based missiles, but was informed that a blockade was an "act of war", Dad wrote the first draft of what became the "Cuban Quarantine Declaration". He thus rewrote international law such that a "quarantine" was defined to mean a blockage of specific materials (missiles), considered an "act less than war." He received the Legion of Merit for his contributions to the nation during the Cuban Missile Crisis.

When I was in Cub Scouts, Dad took the "Pack" on Navy ships as field outings. I began to imagine myself as Captain of a warship. Too many John Wayne movies, I guess. Dad was a great influence on me and my career. He taught me his code of honor long before I encountered the same thing at the Naval Academy. He didn't live to see me in command, but after I made Eagle Scout, somehow, I think he knew I'd get there. I learned from Dad how to discipline my mind, set objectives and focus on them. We also caught a lot of fish together.

My mother was a part of the large Carney family that

were "truck farmers" in Norfolk County's "Churchland" area. She followed Dad to duty in Trinidad just before World War II. Dad was involved in the pre-war negotiations with England that traded some of the U.S. Navy's older destroyers for bases (Trinidad was one of he bases). He was also assigned as one of the officers at the Trinidad Naval Base in the Caribbean Sea.

We lived on that tropic isle until the outbreak of the war after Pearl Harbor. I don't remember much of it, as I was only a few years old, but Mom had strong memories of her time there with Dad. After Pearl Harbor, the Navy flew Mom and I back to Florida on a PBY "flying boat" and we took a train back to Portsmouth.

I was fortunate to have great parents and an adventurous childhood.

*****

In high school, I made good grades and met my love and future wife, Phyllis Garris. I remember the day a friend of mine said "I know some girls who'll go water skiing with us." We went to Phyllis' house, picked her and her friend up, and went on a waterskiing adventure that turned out to last a lifetime.

Phyllis was a beautiful brunette with brown eyes and a pony tail. I was the envy of the many who considered her the "prettiest girl in our school". She turned out to be a wonderful Navy wife. Not many Naval Academy graduates marry their high school sweethearts, as it's a tough four years there, unlike any normal dating scene in college.

We had two children, Robert Bruce (later a naval aviator who retired as a Commander) and Carolyn, who took after her mother in becoming an artist.

*****

I played football for the Churchland High School "Truckers". We had a tough, unrelenting task master for a coach, Charles E. "Shotgun" Brown. We had a "perfect season" in the fall of 1954 when we went undefeated, untied and un-scored upon, and won the State Championship in our Division.

I remember one game when we were leading 60-0. Like the line in the movie "Butch Cassidy and the Sundance Kid", an opposing player asked me "who are you guys, anyway?" Shotgun had us in such good shape, wanting to win so badly (to lose would discredit our coach), and so disciplined that the games were almost an afterthought. The real tough times were at practice when Shotgun would "see what you had!"

Along with my Dad, Shotgun was an influence in my life. He taught me how to survive tough times, give my all and win.

*****

At the U.S. Naval Academy in Annapolis, Maryland, I was thrust into a world where everyone was smart and tough. I was seventeen years old and in a strange, new and very competitive world. You lived by the honor code, you "told it like it is", you kept your chin up in the most difficult situations and persevered. In between all that, you managed to have some fun.

I was an average student and set my sights on graduating, getting a commission and marrying Phyllis. I got my share of demerits along the way, but managed to fulfill those goals. I graduated in the middle of the class and was commissioned Ensign, U.S. Navy in June of 1960. Soon thereafter, Phyllis and I were married and set off on a honeymoon that would end with me reporting aboard my first destroyer, USS JONAS INGRAM (DD-938) in Mayport, Florida. The adventure of our life together began.

*****

It wasn't long before INGRAM deployed. It was a six month cruise around the continent of Africa called Southern Atlantic Amity (SOLANT AMITY). It was a pure "show the flag" mission that took us to places like Cape Town and Durban, South Africa, Mombasa, Kenya and a lot of places of which I had never heard. I remember going into Durban. We were the first U.S. Navy ship to visit there since World War II. As we steamed by the breakwater, there was a woman standing on the rocks dressed as the Statue of Liberty singing "God Bless America". Things have changed.

During this first cruise, it became clear to me that an officer's reputation was built on how he "carried himself", his knowledge of the ship, the manner in which he dealt with his men (fair but firm) and above all, his ability to handle the ship. You did well if you were a "team player," but it also served you well to find a way to stand out among the crowd. Confidence was the key. You had to know your job well enough to be confident in yourself, and have your juniors and seniors feel confident in you.

I worked hard to learn all the lessons well. I did not, on my first ship, have much opportunity to handle the ship. That would change when I reported to my next ship, LAFFEY, where I became the OOD upon whom the Captain called in most situations.

*****

I achieved command at the relatively early age of thirty-five. In the fourteen years since I graduated from the Naval Academy, I had served aboard four destroyers; U.S.S. JONAS INGRAM (DD-938) as Gunnery officer, USS LAFFEY (DD-724) as Weapons Officer and Operations Officer, my first tour aboard RICKETTS as Weapons Officer, and USS LAWRENCE (DDG-4) as Executive Officer.

After my tour aboard JONAS INGRAM, I attended and graduated with Class Number Two at the U.S. Naval Destroyer School, Newport, Rhode Island. After my tour aboard LAFFEY, I attended the U.S. Naval Post Graduate School in Monterey, California and graduated with a Master of Science in Electrical Engineering. Between my first tour aboard RICKETTS and LAWRENCE, I did a 16 month tour with NAVAL FORCES, VIETNAM and an assignment with the NAVAL ORDNANCE SYSTEMS COMMAND in Washington, D.C.

*****

I took command of RICKETTS in March of 1974. I relieved Commander (later Vice Admiral) Frank Donovan, a competent and well liked officer. A week after taking command, tugs towed my ship "dead stick" (no power) to the Norfolk Naval Ship Yard for a thirteen month complex overhaul. All of the ship's equipment was to be overhauled and updated. This was an inconspicuous beginning for a new Captain who yearned to "go down to the sea in ships".

I resolved to become an engineering manager for a while. It wasn't all bad. In spite of its name, Norfolk Naval Ship Yard is in Portsmouth, Virginia, the city where I grew up, the city where my family went back several hundred years. I was home.

Phyllis and I had our two children by this time. It would be nice to be near them for awhile after many deployments and two tours in Vietnam (one in country, that is, in Viet Nam, and one as Executive Officer of LAWRENCE, deployed to Vietnam).

I would have to disassemble much of my ship, overhaul its machinery, reassemble it and pass a number of tough tests and trials to "get the sticker on my window" that made RICKETTS a fully operational destroyer.

I also faced the test every new Captain faces; setting the standards for the crew, showing them what I expected, and setting the "tone" for the ship. Always difficult, I anticipated that it would be much more difficult in a shipyard environment. I was right.

I had served in all departments except supply and engineering. Before I took command, I requested and received orders to attend an engineering refresher course at Newport, Rhode Island. I felt qualified to assume command. Years of observing my commanding officers, the things they did right and the things I thought they did wrong, all came together now. I was the Captain.

*****

No matter how qualified, assuming command is a sobering experience. Suddenly, you are "the man". On your ship, you are responsible for everything—everything! The buck goes no further than you. Yes, you report to a Squadron Commodore, but the ship and the crew are your responsibility. When you leave or return to the ship, flags are lowered or raised and boat gongs are sounded. The perks are nice but in no way are they commensurate with the awesome responsibility. You aren't just a CEO; you're the leader of a moving fighting machine full of fuel oil, ammunition and Sailors that frequently stands purposefully into danger.

One of the things I had observed from experience about "setting the tone" was that it is a mistake, after assuming command, to have a wardroom meeting to tell the officers "how it's going to be." It doesn't work. At best, the reaction is "we'll see". At worst, it alienates the officers right at the get-go. You have to SHOW them how it's going to be through your actions. A new Captain has one or two weeks to do that. If he doesn't, he loses it.

And so, I began to "set the tone." I knew what I wanted. I also knew that the American Sailor will give you what you want if you demand it and match your demand with fairness and concern. Looking back at it now, I acknowledge that all this occurred before the days of "political correctness" that have beset the Navy in recent years. In those days, within reason, you could call a dirtbag a dirtbag, and that was that.

*****

I had thought long and hard about command at sea. My philosophy was that one has to demand high standards, but balance that with a real care for the crew and their families. In short, you could ask for a lot if you gave a lot in return.

My methodology was to "never walk by a mistake" and

"never pass by an opportunity to help a Sailor." After all those years aboard destroyers, I knew how it "should be'." I suppose I walked by some mistakes, but not on purpose. And, I believe I helped many Sailors, perhaps not all I could have. But my intent, I believe, was clear.

I knew that it paid off to empower the officers. Liberty (going ashore) is one of the most valuable things to Sailors. They'll give you everything they have on the job, but they want their time ashore too. On most destroyers, the XO controls liberty. It is also controlled by a rigid schedule in which the Sailors must be aboard ship (example: 0730 to 1600). I moved control of the Sailor's liberty down a notch and allowed the Department Heads to control the working hours for their department. I told them, listen to the Chiefs and get the work done that needs to be done; then let your men go ashore. My way of controlling liberty was to hold the Department Heads accountable for the readiness of their men and equipment and meeting objectives we set together in a timely way.

I would go to the bridge, even when in dry dock and "look down" to see "what was going on." I remember seeing a Sailor on watch smoking a cigarette. Careful to always test the chain of command, I rang up the Executive Officer.

"Hey, XO. Have you authorized the forward brow sentry to smoke on watch?"

A short silence, followed by, "No Sir". I didn't have to say more.

My first Executive Officer was Lieutenant Commander Dave Ricketts. He was the nephew of Admiral Claude V. Ricketts for whom the ship was named. I knew that he was a friend of Commodore Schultz, my boss. They had served together in the Pentagon. Soon after I assumed command, Dave came to my cabin, knocked, and came in.

Dave was a very religious minded, serious guy who had dedicated his life to the Navy. He and Kay, his wife, were "all Navy." I felt lucky to have them, so his next words were a bit of a shock.

"Captain, I don't know if I can work for you," said Dave in a solemn voice. "You want too much, too fast."

"Dave, I'm asking for things to be the way they should be. You know that."

"Yes Sir, but it's all coming too fast."

"Go home and think it over, Dave."

"Yes Sir."

Dave left the cabin.

Later, when I was a Squadron Commander, I would tell my Commanding Officers that the most important relationship on the ship was that between the Commanding Officer (CO) and the XO. If that worked the ship would do well. If not, dissension between those two would poison the whole ship's atmosphere. On my first ship, I had encountered such a situation. I didn't understand it then, but by this time it was clear to me.

It is the XO's job to "figure out" the CO and adapt to what is necessary to support him. I found that out when I worked as XO for Captain Pete Fiedler aboard LAWRENCE.

Pete, a nuclear propulsion trained officer, was a tough, demanding task master who once observed to me that "you can't argue with a man who's right." He demanded nothing but the best, and he was "right". It didn't take me long to discover that Pete was not a "people person," and I had to figure out how to meet his demands and fill that void as best I could.

Pete was relieved by Commander Dick Coolbaugh, a great C.O. who had more "people" skills. Adjustment to Dick's command style was a major change from that of Pete. Somehow, I managed to find the key to supporting both. I learened different things about being "the Captain" from both of them.

The next morning, Dave was back. "Captain, I'm okay with it."

"Good. By the way, did you authorize the Chief Engineer to exempt the Wardroom passageway from mounting hatch spanner wrenches?"

Dave gritted his teeth. I even got a half smile out of him. He went off to solve that problem. He "figured me out", solved many more problems, became an excellent Executive Officer and went on to command his own ship.

He later told me that he adopted the same methods when he was in command. He had a very successful command tour and went on to make Captain. We were good friends throughout our careers.

The Captain owns the bridge and calls the shots. The XO runs the ship the way the Captain wants it run. If these two gentlemen don't get along for whatever reason, the ship will suffer. Dave and I worked it out.

*****

I used small things to show that I would never knowingly "walk by a mistake." Once the officers and crew understood that principle, the big things would take care of themselves.

I was also doing this, I believe, in an even tempered way. I had seen my share of CO's and XO's who were "screamers". That doesn't work. As I liked to tell my officers, "to get things done right requires constant, unrelenting pressure with a friendly smile."

When something went wrong, it did no good to scream and put on a show. The "wrong" likely occurred because I didn't set the standards in that area high enough and demand that they be met. That's where an officer proves his "steel", not with anger and mock toughness.

Later, once I got the ship to sea, and we had been at sea for a long, boring time, the XO came to me and said "Captain, the crew is bored. You need to give 'em something to talk about."

So I threw a little tantrum there for effect. I think the crew knew what was going on. You can't fool the American Sailor!

*****

When I was Weapons Officer aboard RICKETTS as a Lieutenant, my CO was Commander Tom Mullane. Tom was an extremely competent officer and a nice guy, but he had an Irish temper that occasionally got the best of him. His XO, Lieutenant Commander Bill Vollmer was more even tempered and provided some relief.

Soon after I took over the Weapons Department, we went to Bloodsworth Island in the Chesapeake Bay for gun fire support exercises (gun fire support is support of troops ashore with the ship's guns). It was a disaster. We couldn't hit anything. The Captain chewed me out up and down. We left Bloodsworth and went back to Norfolk.

When the guns are as inaccurate as I found them to be at Bloodsworth, it's usually because of erosion of the gun bore due to the firing of excessive rounds. Each gun barrel has a "life" and at some point has to be replaced. I had checked all the gunnery logs and confirmed that the barrels had not reached the end of their life. But, they were acting like they had. Somewhere, somehow, the records had not been accurately maintained. But this was no time to mourn over poor records.

I went into action and immediately requested "regunning" (replacement of the barrels with new ones). Once this was accomplished, we went back to Bloodsworth, fired and did well.

Later, when I took command of RICKETTS from Frank Donovan, I received a letter from Tom. It said, "it pays to not fire your Weapons Officer; he may be your relief!"

Tom had a sense of humor to go with his Irish temper.

*****

In March of 1968, when I was Weapons Officer, RICKETTS was on the way to the Mediterranean Sea and stopped in San Miguel, Ponta Delgada, Azores to refuel. While moored to the pier during refueling, some 3,000 gallons of fuel oil was accidentally pumped over the side into the harbor. Uh Oh!

We had a Division Commander embarked, Captain William R. Glaser. The Commodore was a professional and competent officer, but when his temper took over, he wa a "screamer". Having two senior officers aboard with volatile tempers made the scenes on the bridge interesting at times. Needless to say, neither the Captain nor the

Commodore was pleased with the oil spill.

Bill Vollmer quickly organized the ship. We put over booms to contain the oil and set up an all hands bucket brigade that scooped the oil from the harbor and dumped it into a rented tanker on the pier.

I made up a ditty to the tune of "We Sailed on the Sloop John B", a popular folk song. There are about seven verses. It went like this;

We came on the can Claude V,
My First Lieutenant and Me,
Round Ponta Delgada we did roam,
And spilled us some oil.
What a turmoil,
I feel so broke up,
I want to go home.

Oh woe to the old Claude V,
Got oil all over the sea,
Send for the bucket brigade,
And dip me some oil,
What a turmoil,
The oil was black and the
Water was cold in the hole.

I'm not sure the Captain or the Commodore appreciated my creativity, but I survived.

After a year aboard, Captain Mullane called me to his cabin and showed me the top notch fitness report he wrote on me. He told me, "Vice Admiral Zumwalt, my CO when I was Weapons Officer on USS DEWEY (DLG-45), is going to Vietnam to be COMMANDER, NAVAL FORCES, VIETNAM (COMNAVFORV). He called and asked if I had any hard charging officers who could be on his staff. Want to go?"

It was quite a surprise. I went home and called my father. At the time, my brother, David who had graduated from West Point in 1967, was in Vietnam with the 11th Armored Cavalry.

My Dad's reply was, "Don't ever tell your mother I said

this, but you should go. Bud Zumwalt is a 'comer'."

He was right, as Admiral Zumwalt later became the youngest Chief of Naval Operations that the Navy appointed.

So, I volunteered for Vietnam. Within 24 hours I received orders to the staff of COMNAVFORV via counterinsurgency training school at Little Creek, Virginia.

Later, Tom and I served in Vietnam together and maintained a high mutual respect.

I owe Tom Mullane a lot.

*****

Counterinsurgency training was made up of classes, physical conditioning, and a week in the wilderness for survival, evasion, resistance and escape (SERE) training. All I can remember from the classes was an old Chief who informed us with great glee that "there are a hundred kinds of snakes in Vietnam; ninety-nine are poisonous and the other one eats you alive!" Words of wisdom.

We were taken to Fort Lee near Petersburg, Virginia. It was December 1968. Snow was on the ground. My daughter, Carolyn, had just been born so my decision to volunteer for Vietnam was not overly popular on the home front. We were put out into the forest.

I was a Lieutenant and the senior man in our group. I had mostly a bunch of Seabees (CB, for construction battalion) with me (about 12). We were given warm clothing and sleeping bags and told to build a survival lean-to, which we did. The cold was brutal; down to about twenty-two degrees Fahrenheit.

They gave us a chicken which was so skinny it must have been pre-starved just for us. No one had killed a chicken before. Like many Americans, the Sailors were used to chicken in plastic wrappers at the grocery store. I had spent many summer on my grandparent's farm growing up, and watched my grandfather kill a chicken for Sunday dinner every week. So, I prepared to dispatch the chicken. Then, one of the Sailors volunteered for the duty, and he saw to it. We boiled that thing for hours trying to make a broth, but it didn't provide much sustenance.

The tale circulated that once a dog ran through the area during SERE training, and later, all they found was its collar. We were cold and hungry. We survived on wild onions and sassafras tea.

The next day we were raided by "Red Force" players. They let us escape and we were told to hike to an objective shown on our maps. Off we went into the snowy forest, doing land navigation with terrain maps and a compass.

We came to a river. How to get across? I took my frozen group down river until we found a beaver dam and started across. I hadn't counted on an incompetent beaver.

CRASH!

We fell through the beaver dam in water up to our knees. We struggled to the other side, took off our boots and put on dry socks. But my feet never felt warm for a long, long time.

That night, we pushed on to our objective. I'll never forget it. There was a full moon. The bare branches of all the trees were coated with ice and icicles that reflected the moonlight in a mysterious and beautiful luminescent, blue color. Up and down hills we went through this surreal landscape.

We saw a light ahead. As we came closer, we could see it was a bonfire. We headed for it. The instructors had built a fire to temporarily warm us. Then it was back into the forest toward our objective.

The next day, we were recaptured by Red Force and thrown into a prison camp surrounded by barbed wire. Once inside, we were beat up (just a little) and subjected to other indignities that simulated the kind of treatment we might expect in the hands of an enemy.

There was a fire in the center of the camp which we huddled around. Red Force ordered us to strip off all our clothes, and then moved us gradually away from the fire every time we refused to "confess" our sins against them. Man! That was cold.

A Red Force Player pulled me aside. "What's the matter with you? Aren't you going to take up for your men?"

At that point I was confused and very cold. I took the cue and loudly objected to our mistreatment. After a while, an American flag was broken and a loudspeaker blared out the national anthem. We were freed.

They gave us blankets and C-rats (combat rations, in cans). C-rats never tasted so good. My feet didn't thaw out until I had been in Saigon for several days.

*****

I became the Logistics Plans and Operations Officer on the Commander, U.S. Naval Forces, Vietnam (COMNAVFORV) staff. I was in charge of the basing system in III and IV Corps for our River Patrol Boats (PBRs), Swift Boats (PCFs) and Armored Riverine Craft.

I hitched rides on Army helicopters out to the Mekong Delta and reconnoitered locations for our bases as the PBRs moved into new territory.

In Saigon, I lived in an old hotel that had been transformed into a barracks for officers. At night, I would sit in the little restaurant on top of the hotel and watch the area on the outskirts of Saigon light up with gunfire and bombs. Korean and Filipino girls would sing American rock n' roll songs on Saturday night. They knew the sounds well. I was never sure they knew the words.

Frequently, I would hitch a ride on Admiral Zumwalt's helicopter as he went out to the various bases for briefings and "see the boss" trips. So, I got to know the Admiral fairly well. He would always promise the base commanders some additional supplies or weapons. It was my job to go back to Saigon and take the action to make sure they got what the Admiral promised.

After a while, I got fed up with this existence. I was seeing action, but wasn't "in it". In June of 1969, I submitted a letter asking that I be relived of staff duty and given command of a river patrol boat squadron.

Soon thereafter, Admiral Zumwalt asked me to become

his Aide and Flag Secretary. It was not what I had asked for, but who could turn down an opportunity like that! But there was a catch. I would have to extend three months in country to take the job.

I took the job, and tried my best to explain it to Phyllis, who was at home with our two children. Once again, it didn't go over too well, but Phyllis absorbed the blow and we pressed on. She was a wonderful lady and wife. She went through my entire Navy career and stuck by my side. It was hard on her at times. But she shared the excitement of it all with me, and our marriage survived.

As the Admiral's Aide, I now went everywhere he went. I was responsible for his schedule, his security in a war zone, and following up on whatever action he wanted taken. Vice Admiral Elmo R. (Bud) Zumwalt, Jr. was a soft spoken, highly energetic man who was willing to try a hundred things, be satisfied if ten of them worked, and was man enough to absorb the flak for those that didn't. He demonstrated those traits later when he became Chief of Naval Operations (CNO). In Vietnam, he was fun to work for, demanded the most, and got results.

I moved into the Admiral's quarters in an old French plantation house next to Naval Headquarters. Later, he would give me a silver tray that was engraved, "Presented To LCDR Robert C. Powers, USN, counselor and advisor in war." That meant a lot to me.

I learned much from Bud Zumwalt, and we remained friends even after we had both retired from the Navy. He was another man who had a strong influence on me, along with Dad and Shotgun. Most of all I learned from him how important loyalty "up" and loyalty "down" is to a leader. Secondly, I learned how much one man can accomplish if he sets his mind and energies to it. I also learned what courage truly is, not only on a battlefield in the face of an enemy, but also in facing and making the tough decisions that confront you. This all served me well throughout my career.

This is not a book about Vietnam, but a few incidents will reveal the nature of our operations and my job with the Admiral, and how it all was a part of "getting ready."

*****

Soon after I took over, the Admiral told me that the Stewards (Sailors who took care of the Admiral's house and prepared meals) were keeping Vietnamese girls in the walled and guarded compound. He suggested that I have them removed.

Not one to fool around, I ordered the Chief Steward to have the girls removed from the compound.

Soon thereafter, the Admiral and I were returning from a trip to a riverine base. We started up the stairway to our rooms to change from field greens to khakis. We were interrupted by Mr. Ho, the Vietnamese House Boy (an honorable and professional little man who took good care of us). He ran down the stairs chasing a girl, shouting at her angrily in Vietnamese.

He had gone to my room to "lay out" my khakis. I told him many times to just do that for the Admiral, but he insisted, and who was I to cause him to "lose face"?

Upon entering my room, he found the girl there waiting for me with my loaded Navy .38 caliber revolver (I had worn my .45 caliber semi-automatic pistol on the trip to the base).

No doubt, Mr. Ho saved my life, or at least serious injury, that day. That girl was mad at being forced to leave the compound and intended to do me harm. My eternal thanks go to Mr. Ho.

Soon after that, I called the Marine General's staff in I Corps and asked for a Marine to serve as the Admiral's bodyguard (there was some self-preservation also involved in the request). A Marine sergeant reported to me after a few days (I wish I could remember his name, but it's been awhile). He was a tough, well qualified young man who thereafter accompanied the Admiral and me most of the time.

Whew!

*****

I had been on the fringe of a lot of action by the PBRs, Armored Riverine Boats and Coastal Swift Boats, but never got into the action. I was determined to go on patrol and see some action.

The Admiral and I went to a floating base in the Nam Cam Peninsula of the Mekong Delta called "SEAFLOAT". It was strategically positioned to send out patrols that blocked enemy logistic movement in the southern delta. I had helped conceive it and make it happen in my previous job on the staff. The Sergeant was with us.

The Admiral received his briefings and talked to the Sailors. He was determined to spend the night there. We finally saw him off to his bunk. SEAFLOAT was built on pontoons anchored in the middle of a fast moving river, and was well guarded, so I felt comfortable leaving the Admiral there. The night was filled with the "thump" of anti-swimmer charges thrown from the base and forty millimeter grenades fired randomly at positions on the nearby shore (to "flush out" any Viet Cong that might try to approach the base)

The Sergeant and I negotiated a place on a "Swift Boat" (PCF, or Patrol Boat Fast, a 50 foot coastal patrol boat armed with .50 caliber machine guns, 12.7 mm machine guns, grenade launchers and an 81 mm mortar) that was going on a patrol along one of the many canals near SEAFLOAT. It was a spooky night (most were) as we motored down narrow canals, jungle and mango swamps on each side of us. It was dark with little moon.

We stopped and set up a "water-borne guard post" (a politically correct name for an ambush position) somewhere along the canal. The crew, the Sergeant and I were all in full battle gear with M-16 rifles.

Nothing much was moving, except the mosquitoes. Hordes of them feasted on my hands and face. It was hot and sticky which made it worse. Long hours went by. The surrounding jungle was dark and thick with vegetation. Every shadow loomed as a threat.

We didn't run into any Viet Cong that night, and went back the next morning to find a fresh Admiral raring to go. We had to work hard to hide where we'd been and how tired we were. But, I had at least tasted what it was like out there and what our men went through night after night.

Later, we visited a base on the Vinh Te Canal near Cambodia. Again, the Sergeant and I negotiated a place on a Swift Boat Patrol along the canal. As we were about to embark on the Swift Boat, Admiral Zumwalt showed up.

The Admiral had a soft but demanding way of speaking. "Where're you going, Bob?"

"Uh—out on patrol, Admiral."

"Thought you fooled me back there on SEAFLOAT, didn't you?" said the Admiral with a sly grin.

"Well, no. Admiral. I mean…"

"I'm going tonight."

"Sir, you can't go out there…"

"Who's the Admiral around here, Bob?"

The Sergeant was getting a kick out of all this.

"Okay, Admiral."

I turned to the Sergeant.

"Sergeant, please remove all signs of rank that the Admiral wears or has with him."

Now the Sergeant was really grinning.

"Aye aye, Sir."

So, the Sergeant took the Admiral's ID card and tore the three stars off his collar. He ripped the name "ZUMWALT" off the Admiral's greens.

We embarked on the SWIFT Boat and spent the night patrolling the Vinh Te Canal near Cambodia. We saw a lot of action, but didn't get into any. The flyboys were bombing something on a nearby mountain. It was all lit up like a Christmas tree. There was a firefight a few klicks (kilometers) down the canal from us. We could hear M-16s and AK-47s.

After a while the action died down. We spent the rest of the night fighting the mosquitoes. Just as well, as I was having trouble thinking how I was going to explain to the Chief of Staff how I let the Admiral get into a firefight. That would have been a tough one!

*****

After Vietnam, I went to Washington and served as Executive Assistant to one of the best men I've ever known, Rear Admiral Mark W. Woods. Mark was COMMANDER, NAVAL ORDNANCE SYSTEMS COMMAND. He commanded all Navy programs that had to do with shipboard weapons. If I had to be on shore duty, there wasn't a better place than working for Mark.

For two years I worked to get the AEGIS weapon system, the Mark 48 torpedo, the HARPOON missile, and a new five inch gun, among other things, into the fleet. I learned how the Washington bureaucracy worked. I had time with my family.

I learned from Mark the true meaning of "officer and gentleman". He was both, in all ways. Mark had a decided influence on me.

Then, it was back to the fleet as XO of LAWRENCE, a ship of the same class of destroyers as RICKETTS.

*****

Chapter Four
Overhaul

Dry docks, cranes, whistles, grease, hydraulic oil and air driven paint chipping hammers that beat endlessly in my ears. Mazes of wires and hoses. My ship torn apart. Streams of yard workers in helmets of different colors that signified their trade and position file aboard around the clock.

These are some of my memories of ship yards. But among all that, the Sailors had to live and work, and they were my responsibility.

I walked the decks and spaces of RICKETTS every day to see the Sailors and be seen. One day, while doing this, I stopped to talk to a young Sailor.

"Gee Captain, you get to have all the fun, up there on the bridge and all. I'm stuck down in the engine room watching gauges on the boiler."

"I've been there," I replied, remembering my Midshipman cruise and Destroyer School. "You can put in the work and time to learn enough to stand on the bridge and be Captain. You just have to decide to do it."

"Yes Sir, I never thought about it that way."

*****

It didn't take me long to understand the strengths and weaknesses of my officers. We were in a ship yard, so I couldn't observe and train them in my favorite occupation—ship handling. But I could train them in setting standards and abiding by them. I could train them in engineering project management; managing resources and scheduling objectives. I could teach them quality control and how one must schedule and follow up, and follow up again.

So, I set up a system. I would meet with the XO and the Department Heads and discuss our short and long term objectives. We would discuss what we needed to do to meet those objectives. Then the Department heads would meet with the Division Officers, Chiefs and Leading Petty Officers and create "management by objective" schedules; what we were going to do and what was a reasonable time to complete the task. I reviewed the schedule, adjusted a few things and signed off on it. We held ourselves accountable to that schedule and as a result, got things done. Sometimes we had to extend or reschedule a task, but the important thing was, we each knew what we had to do, all the time. This "system" became a "way of life" aboard RICKETTS and extended beyond the overhaul.

We had an enormous task just making sure that ship yard jobs were accomplished correctly and on time. Good overhauls occur because the Captain and the crew demand it. Problems occur when the Captain and crew lean back and expect the ship yard personnel to "do it all".

In addition to working with the shipyard, we had some big "ship's force" work to do. Among these jobs were cleaning and painting the bilges in four main engineering spaces, ripping up years of "tile on tile" in the ship's passageways and replacing it. We installed new modular bunks and lockers for the crew's berthing spaces, and overhauled hundreds of valves. Not to mention just keeping the ship clean and "squared away" enough for most of the crew to live aboard while the shipyard work was ongoing.

The ship yard Commander at the time was Vice Admiral Joe Williams, a submariner. He was a feisty guy with a wealth of experience. I took him a lot of problems and somehow he found a way to help out.

Ship cleanliness and water tight integrity were major issues. Every day, the ship was invaded by "Yard Birds" to do their overhaul work. In their minds, they were paid to do the work and whatever residue that work caused was "someone else's problem." I fought this one hard and demanded that the ship yard be responsible for cleaning up after its jobs. The XO put into place several programs designed to keep the ship tidy.

A big problem was soft drink cans. They were discarded all over the ship. Finally, we set a policy that canned soft drinks could only be consumed at a designated place on the fantail.

*****

Admiral Williams came to the ship to inspect the work going on in the engine rooms. I showed him the bilges (space between the bottom hull of the ship and the "deck plates", or walkways in the engine rooms). The bilges were filthy from years of neglect. My predecessor, Frank Donovan had started the clean-up process. I intended to finish it. I told Admiral Williams I planned to clean them up to the point where we could "chow down" on them. He cast a skeptical eye my way.

"Tell you what, Captain," said the Admiral, "if you can get those bilges clean enough to pass MY inspection, I'll pay to have them painted."

The Admiral had a discretionary fund to deal with "things that came up", and I assumed he would use that. I took him up on the bet immediately.

"You're on, Admiral."

Before I could complete the overhaul satisfactorily, I had to pass a tough examination from a new set of inspectors whose job was to improve engineering readiness in the force—the dreaded "Propulsion Examining Board (PEB)". I knew that clean bilges and good looking engine rooms boosted a Sailor's pride, which in turn would make everything in the Engineering Department better.

Dave Ricketts and I put our heads together and decided on an unorthodox plan. We would use Sailors from all the ship's Departments (Operations, Weapons, Engineering and Supply) to clean the bilges. We would put Chiefs from all departments in charge of the bilge cleaners (their own Chiefs) so the Engineering Chiefs could spend most of their time on engineering work. We would have a day shift and a night shift. We would buy the men special coveralls with a special "team" name on them. We dreamed up a name which I don't remember, but the idea was to make it a challenge for the men—and the Chiefs, and to develop pride and teamwork.

The key was the Chiefs. I could imagine what a grizzled old Chief Gunner's Mate would have to say about going below to "clean up the Snipe's (nickname for the Engineers) mess".

"XO," said I, "we have to sell it to the Chiefs."

The line would be, "we have to get our "inspection sticker" (the PEB) on the bridge windshield before we can get to sea, operate, shoot and go to some exotic, fun places."

So off went Dave to sell it to the Chiefs. I would follow up later.

The officers lead, establish policy, assume responsibility and conn the ship, but the Chief's make the ship function. The second most important relationship on a ship (the first being that between the CO and XO) is that between the Wardroom Officers and the Chief Petty Officers. They must each understand and respect the other and the role they play. If the Chiefs lose respect for an officer, or the officers in general, the ship suffers. If the officers don't understand the value of the Chiefs and what they do, the ship suffers.

The XO, who is usually about the same age as many of the Chiefs, plays an essential role as a "go-between" for the Officers and the Chiefs. It's a unique relationship. The officers have to be in charge, as they have accepted commissions as naval officers and bear the responsibility. They have the advantage of more education, but have less overall experience. They have to earn the respect of men with much more experience than they have. The Chiefs have to mentor the officers, "keep them out of trouble" and support them, while at the same time acknowledge that the officers are in charge.

The officers have a broad educational background. The Chiefs are experts in their trades. As "old sea dogs", they are the men the Sailors look up to and with whom they have the most contact. The Chiefs are the ones who decide if the "Old Man" (The Captain), the XO and the Wardroom have it all together and deserve the respect of the crew. The Chiefs are the irreplaceable heart of any ship.

Long before there were "Master Chiefs of the Ship", I created one. I went to Chief's Quarters and told them I wanted to have A "Master Chief of the Ship" who would have direct access to me (though he'd better keep the XO cut in) and be the Sailor's representative. I singled out the most senior Master Chief and asked if he wanted the job. Fortunately he did. It worked well, as we shall see.

We won the bet with Admiral Williams and he paid to have the bilges painted. We took a similar approach to other big ship's force jobs. We were team building.

It didn't go without problems. I went out to my car late one evening and found a paint sprayed message on the hood of my car. "Powers sucks!" I went immediately back to the ship and called the Master Chief of the Ship.

"Please go out on the pier and look at my car."

That was all I needed to say. I waited an hour, and went back to my car. The sign was gone and the car was newly polished. No more was said of it.

*****

A Captain must ensure that the officers of his wardroom are "not only capable leaders and mariners" (to quote John Paul Jones), but also that they are gentlemen worthy of respect. It takes time to train and build a better than average wardroom. But you'll never get there if you don't start with good material.

To begin with, the Captain must be honest with himself and the officers, chiefs and crew. He must set a good example. For, when one assumes command, it is a contract between you, your values and the men you lead. The Navy of today has had to "fire" far too many Commanding Officers who have failed to understand this; failed to set a good example..

A Captain has a choice; he can work with what he has, good or bad, or he can weed out the weaknesses before they cause him problems. A Captain who fails to identify and weed out the weaknesses will come to the point where he's not only doing his job but trying to make up for the weak officers. That does not make for a "fun" tour as Commanding Officer. It's also potentially dangerous. Hard as this may be in today's "politically correct" Navy, it still must be done.

My Weapons Officer (WEPS), Lieutenant Mike Weir was a big, happy go lucky guy who worked hard, played hard and sometimes struggled with his responsibilities. I could work with him. My Operations Officer (OPS), Lieutenant Mark Lodge, was an average officer who sometimes displayed a lack of confidence. He might be a problem. Time would tell. Mike and Mark were both doing an adequate job in overhaul. They would be relieved later on in the year.

I learned in working for Admiral Zumwalt that if you keep the pressure on the Bureau of Naval Personnel (BUPERS), they will send you the better officers. Admiral Zumwalt kept me busy doing that for and with him (among many other things). And so I started working BUPERS; the old squeaking wheel in need of grease.

It was different with my Engineer Officer (Chief Engineer, or CHENG) in the ship yard. He was a nice guy. I truly liked him. I knew him in a later occupation and still liked him. But, it became clear to me that he did not have the respect of his Chief Petty Officers.

When the Chief Engineer came to see me about the latest problem, he would always bring a Chief Petty Officer with him "to explain". That doesn't work. Any senior officer will take that as a show of lack of self-confidence, which translates to ability.

The Chief Engineer was a Lieutenant Commander with years of experience as an Engineering Duty Officer (an officer who specializes in engineering) and several degrees from recognized engineering schools. Problem was, he lacked confidence in himself, was not a leader, and his men saw it. I noted to myself that I would have to watch that situation closely. I would work with him—for a while, and see if he'd shape up.

Soon after I took command, it came to my attention that the Main Propulsion Assistant (MPA, the number two man in the engineering department) was having an affair with the Supply Officer's wife. This astounded me. In my set of values, you did not, under any circumstances, have an affair with a shipmate's wife. The concept of "shipmate" is an important one and a more dishonorable situation was not conceivable to me. I discussed the situation with the XO, and he confirmed it.

"Why haven't you done something about it?"

"It's not my place to intervene in a private matter," replied Dave. "Besides, he's the officer that 'keeps it all together' in the Engineering Department. To lose him would be disastrous."

I did not view it that way. I considered it a matter that was at the heart of wardroom morale, and as I have previously written, the morale of the whole ship's crew.

I called Lieutenant Jim Bogart, then the Supply Officer. Jim was a gregarious and hard-working officer who understood all things supply. I liked him and his can do attitude toward everything. When I took command, I told him I expected him to get whatever we needed when we needed it one way or the other. I also told him not to bend the rules without talking to me about it first. I would determine if the rule could or should "be bent".

I also told Jim I wanted to win all the prizes in the fleet for the best chow hall. Chow is an essential morale factor during long, hard days at sea. I remembered long watch hours at GQ as XO of LAWRENCE when we were providing gun fire support to the Marines in Vietnam. Sometimes, that last juicy hamburger was the only thing making up for hours of lost sleep.

Jim was pursuing all these goals well. I couldn't understand why he was putting up with the situation I described.

"What about this situation with the MPA and your wife, Jim?"

"Yes Sir, I know about it."

"Why haven't you done something about it?"

"Captain, I don't want to disrupt the wardroom."

That didn't sit well with me. I called the MPA to my cabin and asked him if he was having an affair with the Supply Corps Officer's wife. He admitted to it. I informed him he had until 1800 hours (about six hours from then) to get off the ship and don't come back. He was truly surprised.

"Where am I supposed to go?"

"Report to the Admiral's staff and tell them I can't use you any longer on this ship."

Now I had to watch the Engineering Department even more closely. The ship was stripped of much of its propulsion machinery. The machinery had gone to the "shops" in the ship yard to be overhauled. New digital weapons computers were being installed. We were busy.

*****

The XO came to me one morning with bad news.

"We have an officer AWOL (Absent Without Leave)."

He told me who it was. I was surprised.

"Well, find him."

The next day, the XO arrived with more on the matter.

"The AWOL Officer called in. He's in a motel, says he wants to talk to you, at the motel. My advice is not to go. I talked to him. He doesn't sound right."

Here was a dilemma.

"What's his problem?"

"He wouldn't say. Just says he wants to talk to you. Don't go, Captain. I'll send the Shore Patrol out there."

If I went, there was some risk. If I sent the Shore Patrol, his career was over.

"I'll go."

"I'll go with you," said Dave.

"No, I need to do this."

I went to the motel and met with the officer. He was distraught, very nervous. He said he had come from a larger ship and wasn't used to the pressure he was experiencing on a destroyer. He was sorry. He wanted to do well, but he couldn't handle it.

I listened to his story. He had personal problems also. After about a half hour, I told him to come back with me and I would approve a request for transfer.

The officer was prior enlisted. On the larger ship, he

could contribute and perhaps be of value. On a destroyer, where it's hustle every day and officers get large responsibility early in their career; it was different than anything he had experienced. It was best for him, the wardroom and the Navy that he go to a larger ship.

At first, he didn't believe I meant what I said. I talked to him another half hour before he agreed to come back with me. Later I learned that he switched his career to Aviation Maintenance Officer and had been promoted.

A Captain is always faced with tough choices. I felt I made the right one in his case.

*****

I arrived at the ship one morning and observed a very large hole in the side. The ship yard had put a hole in my ship to remove a major piece of machinery for overhaul. I walked to the edge of the pier to examine it. The bottom lip of the hole was only a few feet from the waterline. There was no cofferdam in place to keep water out should there be a storm.

I was upset. No one had bothered to get my permission to cut this hole or briefed me on the proper procedure. I kept my temper, but this was as close as I came to screaming at someone.

I called the XO and the Chief Engineer to my cabin, told them to get a cofferdam installed immediately, raise hell with the ship yard about what had occurred, and come back and explain to me why I was not properly briefed and informed.

To make a long and distressing story short, I decided to relieve the Chief Engineer of his duties. This was not done easily. The Bureau of Naval Personnel opposed me. I was told that they could not provide a relief for an indefinite period. I replied that I would manage.

The Damage Control Assistant (DCA) at the time was Lieutenant Junior Grade Ken Sigmon, a competent young officer who exhibited the attributes of leadership that I sought. We (the wardroom) went to happy hour at the Officer's Club and I pinned Lieutenant bars on him and told him he was the Chief Engineer (in those days, the CO had the authority to "frock" an officer, that is, promote him to the rank called for by the billet he occupied).

It came as a surprise to Ken who allowed as how he didn't know a lot about the steam engineering plant. I told him that between the two of us, we knew enough if we trusted and empowered the Engineering Chiefs. What I wanted from him was leadership, organization, accountability and keeping me well informed.

In September, Ensign Rich Celloto reported aboard to relieve Lieutenant Junior Grade Bill Buskirk, who had become the the Main Propulsion Assistant. Rich was an engineering duty officer, technically competent and mature beyond his years, though he looked like he was fresh out of high school. My engineering team was coming together.

This was a time in the Navy when the engineering plants and the men that manned them were our biggest challenge. Ships had been "worn out" in Vietnam with long deployments. The engineering personnel faced excessive hours, fewer duty sections than non-engineers, and little time for family. Enlistments were down and engineering manpower was at a premium. This produced a vicious cycle of fewer reenlistments and below-target recruiting that perpetuated understaffing. I spent a lot of time working with Sailors (particularly engineers) to show them the advantages of reenlisting in the Navy. I appointed a competent Petty Officer to be the ship's career counselor. The ship had a higher than normal re-enlistment percentage as a result.

The leadership task in engineering was challenging. I needed the best officers I could find to assist me in having a top notch engineering capability.

*****

We finished the overhaul on time. New missile and gun fire control digital computers were installed. The ship was completely overhauled, bow to stern, mast to keel. We were proud of what was accomplished. It was a team effort with the Sailors and the Shipyard Workers learning to function well together.

We began the final preparations for the PEB "Light Off Examination (LOE)." We had to pass that examination of our engineering readiness before I could take the ship to sea for test trials.

By this time, the bilges were painted, the valves overhauled, the boilers re-tubed and the major machinery overhauled and tested by the shipyard. The engineers were proud of their "like new" spaces, as were the Sailors from other departments who now had a better idea of what went on "down there" with the Snipes. We put in the final hours of study on engineering procedures and stood by for the dreaded inspectors to arrive.

We faced a "split LOE", that is, two visits by the Propulsion Examining Board. The first visit took place on a Friday in October of 1974. We presented the after fire room and engine room and some of the watch standers. We passed!

The shipyard commander directed us to light off that night to set the pressure on the boiler safety valves. The shipyard was behind schedule and had to catch up. I tried my best to get the engineers off for weekend liberty. They had just passed a very tough inspection, an almost heroic accomplishment that was the culmination of months of hard work and little liberty.

Ken and Rich told the engineers we had to light off. Every Sailor put in a request for Captain's Mast. I called the XO and the Engineer Officer to my cabin.

"I've appealed the decision to light off for the weekend. No joy. I appealed again and received an order to get it done. You should know that. All the men need to know is that I've reviewed the situation and consider it necessary. So go get it done."

So we lit off. Ken and Rich led their men through the situation. It was what was expected of them. They, the engineering Chiefs and the Sailors, all did a great job.

The Second LOE took place a couple of weeks later and examined the other half of the plant. We passed that with only one important discrepancy. That was soon corrected and we were ready for sea trials.

*****

COMMANDER, NAVAL SURFACE FORCES, U.S. ATLANTIC FLEET (NAVSURFLANT) sent me Lieutenant Tom "Mad Dog" Madden as an interim chief engineer until BUPERS could find a permanent replacement. He was an excellent officer and did well in the extremely tight situation into which he was inserted. He was a very big, no-nonsense guy with a lot of authority in his voice.

Thinking ahead, after we finished sea trials, we would be going to the Naval Training Command at Guantanamo Bay, Cuba (GTMO) for two months of refresher training. This meant training in all aspects of being a warship; navigation, operational battle problems, gunnery and missile firings, engineering casualty control exercises and damage control. From experience, I knew that most ships failed damage control. This resulted from inadequate training in fire and flooding drills, and most of all, a demonstrated inability to set "material conditions".

I got Tom and Lieutenant Junior Grade Clarence Hill, the DCA, together and told them to start training hard. Clarence was a rugged young officer known for his determination and spirit. He later commanded a frigate. He got to work and set up an intensive program to train in damage control well before we got out of the shipyard.

A material condition simply means "how well the ship can seal off its various compartments by closing and securing hatches, water tight doors and the like". There are several "conditions"; Material condition XRAY (in port, maximum freedom of passage), YOKE (at sea steaming, prepared to control flooding), ZEBRA (maximum watertight condition used at general quarters and for battle conditions), and WILLIAM (air tight ship to combat chemical weapons).

Every hatch and fitting on the ship was marked with one of these code words to indicate when it could be open and when it must be closed and tightly secured. Training in this area required endless hours of detailed drills. In Refresher Training, an inspector seemed to always find something that had been overlooked or not secured properly. I'd "been there, done that" aboard JONAS INGRAM and LAFFEY.

Tom and Clarence began to drill the crew, determined to do well at GTMO, particularly in setting material conditions, fire fighting and flooding control. I knew that if the ship ever went into battle it was likely to sustain damage and we had to know how to handle it. Likewise, if the ship were in a storm or had any kind of fire or flooding at sea, damage control meant saving the ship or losing it.

I tried to approach getting my ship ready as though I were going into battle. I did not intend that my ship be a "love boat." It was my job to make it a warship.

*****

It was a bright, sunny morning. I was ready to get underway for sea trials. I was on the bridge when Tom came to me and reported that a school of menhaden (a small fish) had somehow gotten into the main seawater intake and clogged the main condenser (where steam exits the steam turbine and is condensed back into feed water in a steam propulsion system). So, for twenty-four hours, the engineers picked fish out of the condenser tubes. It was a nasty job. This was a taste of dealing with the unexpected, something a Captain has to master. Be patient, organize, act quickly and press on.

The next morning, all was ready. A pilot (a licensed individual who takes ships in and out of restricted waters) showed up. I told him he was welcome, but I was going to take the ship out myself. After all, I was a professional and had grown up in Portsmouth and plied all the waters around it in boats of my own. More than that, it was time to demonstrate to the crew that I had confidence in myself and in them.

The ship was port side to the pier, bow out toward the channel. The wind and tide were setting me onto the pier; a classic ship handling situation.

When I served aboard LAFFEY and LAWRENCE, I had obtained a lot of ship handling experience. My Commanding Officers on those ships put trust in me and gave me the conn in most replenishment, restricted water piloting and docking situations. Aboard LAWRENCE, I always had the conn during combat operations in Vietnam, the Captain preferring to be in CIC. But, I was a bit rusty.

Finally, we were ready to get underway. I stood on the bridge. "Single up all lines (the ship moors with doubled lines. This order causes the lines to be made single)." Then, "Take in all lines."

I applied left full rudder to get the screw wash off the rudder to push my stern off the pier. Port engine ahead one third and starboard engine back one third to twist the bow away from the pier. The ship moved sideways, overcoming the wind that set her onto the pier.

"Rudder amidships. All engines ahead two thirds (kick the 5,000 ton ship ahead to keep from being set onto the pier by the wind)."

Then quickly, "all engines ahead one third, left standard rudder." We turned easily into the channel and steamed without incident through Hampton Roads, down Thimble Shoals Channel, passed over the bridge tunnel and proceeded to sea. Not so rusty after all.

In my days of training as an OOD, it was drummed into me that "forehandedness" was a primary attribute of any ship handler. This is a different way of saying "have a plan". It pays to think through all possible situations before you have to deal with them. You'll never think of them all. The unexpected is always there waiting for you. But if you think through most of them, you'll be able to handle the unexpected.

Sea trials went well. We made thirty-five knots for the full power run. The casualty control drills went off without a hitch. I sat on the bridge all night watching my new OODs and getting a feel for their ability and "presence". This was my first chance to observe them at sea. Their knowledge and capability would be gradually discovered. Their "presence" on the bridge tells a lot about them. An OOD has to have an air of confidence that the crew respects. But, their understanding of the ship, it's handling characteristics, relative motion with ships and other objects at sea, and how to remain calm and act in an emergency are the attributes to carefully evaluate.

It was a wonderful few days. I was at sea again, feeling the throb of the ship under me, knowing that it would respond to my every command. I also held my breath. RICKETTS had a 1200 psi steam turbine propulsion system, notorious for its power and danger. One failed valve would send searing hot, superheated steam into the engineering spaces, endangering the lives of all there. One low feed water condition in the boiler could trip the whole plant off line and leave my ship dead in the water. I was confident that we had done a good job in the shipyard and that the yard workers had completed a professional overhaul. After all, we had essentially stripped the ship down to bare metal and rebuilt her. I still held my breath.

*****

Back in port, Captain and Crew felt good about what we had accomplished. With the help of Dave Ricketts, I had built the nucleus of a good wardroom and crew.

In February, 1975, Lieutenant Steve Smith relieved Tom Madden as Chief Engineer. Steve was a tall, professional officer who had served in special boats in Viet Nam. A bachelor, he quickly became a leader in the wardroom in both business and pleasure. He would prove to be a significant asset. My wardroom was building into a fun loving and professional group of officers,

The ship and its crew had proved its worth. It was time to go to sea and become a warship.

*****

We got underway and transited to Naval Ammunition Depot, Earle, New Jersey, arriving on 29 January. New York harbor and the approaches to the ammunition depot are cold, windy and treacherous. My first underway period after the shipyard was a real challenge.

We moored at a very long pier in high winds, but all went well. The weather was bad and getting worse. Once the sea detail was secured, I went to the Officer's Club for dinner.

It wasn't long before the Command Duty Officer called and advised that the wind had picked up considerably and the ship was being pounded against the pier. I went back to the ship immediately.

First big decision; stay at the pier and get pounded or get underway and get out to sea. I looked at the wind swept harbor. A no-brainer. I ordered more fenders be put out. We weathered the night. I was concerned that the ship may have sustained some damage from the pounding. We held a quick inspection inside and out; no damage noted other than losing some fenders and shredding a few more.

The next day we loaded ammunition. We completed the load and were underway on 31 January.

*****

In February, we conducted training in the Virginia Capes Operations Area. Here, I began my policy that we would shoot the guns every time we got underway, conditions permitting. My philosophy was that to function properly when needed, everything must be worked as much as possible. If I ever had to shoot something, I was going to make sure I was ready. Always.

The motor whaleboat and the gig (Captain's boat) engines were started every day and reported to me. The firing circuits on the guns were checked every day. Transmission checks between the fire control systems and the guns were held every day. Damage control drills (fire, flooding, etc.) were held every day. And so forth.

*****

We were back at the Destroyer-Submarine (DESSUB)

Piers in Norfolk. The shipyard was behind us. The Propulsion plant was ready. Radars were tuned. Guns and missiles made ready. Ammunition loaded. We loaded stores and had a few last weeks with our families.

*****

In mid-March, we were underway for Port Everglades (Fort Lauderdale), Florida for Weapons Acceptance tests. Then on to Andros Islands in the Bahamas for sonar tests and firing of exercise torpedoes.

*****

We arrived in Roosevelt Roads, Puerto Rico on 26 March to prepare for missile test firings. The next day, GQ was set and the complex process of firing a missile began. It's not like the movies. It doesn't just "happen" when the CO says "fire" and the Weapons Officer pulls the trigger. Many Sailors spend long hours checking the radars, fire control systems, launcher and missiles.

In CIC, we got the word that the target drone was launched. Radars tracked the drone. The cone shaped fire control radars sent a pencil beam of energy out to "paint" the drone and reflect back to the missile homing receiver, The missile "saw" the pencil beam and followed it.

The word came to me on the bridge. "Bogey (simulated hostile air target) ALFA approaching, range thirty thousand yards. Target range all clear."

"Very well."

At this point, all the training conducted to date becomes immensely important. As CO, you have to have confidence in all the Officers and Sailors manning the many stations involved. Fire Contolmen. Gunners Mates. Radarmen. Range Safety Officers. Electricians. Communications Personnel. If I'd done my job "getting ready", all would be well.

"Permission to bring one missile to the rail Sir."

"Permission granted."

Near the ship's stern, a STANDARD MISSILE ran up

the launcher rail from the magazine below. The launcher spun to aim at the incoming drone.

"Request permission to fire, Captain."

"Fire."

The missile roared away from the launcher. The first time you're near one of these missiles when it launches, it's a shock. It is LOUD! It blasts your senses as it ROARS away.

Tension. Will it hit the drone? 5-4-3-2-1--

A fiery ball in the sky. A tumbling drone.

The cheer in CIC could be heard on the bridge. The phone talker on the bridge had a big smile on his face,

"Direct Hit, Captain."

"Very well."

I wanted to cheer, too. But, I was going to be "cool". After all, they were supposed to hit. Every one of them. That's what I expected. What I demanded,

"Pass the word. Well done,"

*****

We were ready to sail for GTMO.

*****

Chapter Five
Guantanamo Bay

We sailed for Guantanamo Bay (GTMO), Cuba on 31 March. We were on our way to the U.S. Naval Base there to engage in "Refresher Training", required of every ship after a long overhaul. It was a balmy trip to the Caribbean. I sat on the bridge planning training, keeping an eye on my OODs and thinking about GTMO and its challenges. We slowed for a while and allowed the crew to cook burgers and fish off the fantail in the azure waters. Nothing caught, but a good break.

I remembered being at GTMO for refresher training aboard JONAS INGRAM (as an Ensign). In those days, ships mostly anchored in the bay when they were not at sea for training exercises. At anchor, it was not unusual to glance over the side and see a twelve foot hammerhead shark basking in the sun waiting for something to be thrown overboard. Swimming at anchor was not a popular sport.

We rode in the whaleboat to get ashore, or if we were lucky, we might hitch a ride in the Captain's gig. At the fleet officer's landing, there was a small wharf with a white roof over it. It was reported to us that once not long ago an ensign had fallen into the water there and been bitten in a strategically undesirable place by "Charlie the Barracuda", who lived under the wharf. Surely Charlie was there even today waiting for some clumsy ensign to part the waters.

There was a long set of stairs that went up to the officers club. At the club, we spent hours playing "liar's dice" and lying beside the pool hoping some shapely woman would show up. There were tales of nurses who loved ensigns, but somehow they never appeared when I was there.

We would drink "One Eyed Indian", a Cuban beer, or Heineken's for twenty-five cents a bottle. Or, for the more adventurous, there was Cuban rum. You could get a little tipsy as long as you made it to officer's call the next morning. Sometimes, the rest of the day after a night at the club felt like you were walking around on numb stumps. But somehow, we all got through it.

One afternoon, the 1 MC announced, "Now all you en-swines (ensigns) who have the guts to go to the club with the Executive Officer, muster on the fantail." A few of us mustered and later regretted it.

Each morning, it was early reveille and out to sea for training exercises. We spent most of the day at GQ. My GQ station in those days was in the gun director or at gun control above the bridge. The days were long and hot. I could still taste the salt and grime on my tongue.

JONAS INGRAM was in GTMO in 1960 after the Castro revolution had placed Fidel Castro in power. The U.S. sought to protect its rights to the base. For several nights I sat in the gun director with orders to track (or possibly take under fire) any ship or boat that came out of the Cuban waters to the north of the base. This was my first taste of being in a potentially combat situation.

Engineering drills seemed endless. The training instructors would impose an array of different casualties on the ship and grade us on how we reacted and recovered; low water in the boiler, loss of vacuum in the main condenser, high water in the boiler, loss of main feed pump, on and on.

Gunnery exercises. Aircraft would tow target "sleeves" near the ship. I would track it with the director. Guns would boom. Cork, sulfur and cordite filled the air. Then the heat as the Cuban sun baked the metal skin of the gun director as we waited for another target.

And of course, we failed damage control.

In October 1962, I was Weapons Officer on LAFFEY. We were scheduled to go to GTMO for refresher training, but the Cuban missile crisis intervened. Instead, we did our refresher training in the waters off Norfolk, and in between exercises patrolled the entrance to Chesapeake Bay for possible intrusion by Soviet submarines. There was a concern that the Russians might try to mine the waters all U.S. Navy ships passed through on the way to the Naval Station at Norfolk.

It was a tense time, as no one knew whether or not we might see a mushroom cloud over Norfolk where our families were. It was also a frustrating time because our fellow destroyers had raced to the Caribbean to intercept Soviet ships bound for Cuba carrying medium range ballistic missiles. But, we had to do the training. It was the same as GTMO less the heat. Fortunately for all concerned, the Soviets backed down and withdrew their missiles.

I was determined to not let RICKETTS fail damage control, and so we drilled and drilled and drilled at setting material conditions and holding fire and flooding exercises. The then Damage Control Assistant, Lieutenant Junior Grade Clarence Hill, was kept very busy. Clarence was an athletic young man who would charge hard at any target; just give him one. He kept the Damage Control Petty Officers (DCPO) in all of the ship's divisions hard at it. He went on to have a command of his own as a Commander.

Then, damage control equipment started to disappear; spanner wrenches, fire hose nozzles and the like. Dave came to me one morning in my cabin with bad news.

"Captain, the Phantom DCPO has struck again, this time big time."

The "Phantom DCPO" was the name the crew had given to the thief. I was fed up with it.

"What now?"

"The P-250 fire pump in the port break (main deck just under the bridge where there was a shield in the superstructure against weather from the bow) is missing."

"He must be a big guy if he can heft that thing over the side."

"Yes Sir. I'm trying to get a line on who it is."

"Have the Master Chief of the Command come up here."

Dave disappeared for about ten minutes and returned with the Master Chief.

"Master Chief, you need to get the word out that this Phantom DCPO guy is endangering the ship. That's not the way shipmates act. Shipmates take care of each other.

I know you know that."

"Yes Sir, Captain."

"Someone on the ship knows who this dirtbag is. I want to know by tomorrow morning."

"I got it, Captain."

Three hours later, I had a name. I couldn't prove that the Sailor named had thrown the gear over the side. But he was a well known slaggard. I called Dave back. I handed him the slip of paper with the name on it.

"Dave, I want this guy watched, night and day."

Needless to say, the Phantom DCPO thefts stopped. Where before he had been a subject of humor to many of the crew (damn damage control drills are driving me nuts, etc.), the Master Chief had turned the tables on him. The Phantom DCPO was no longer a shipmate; he was a subject of ridicule. There is no more powerful punishment than rejection by your peers, and he found that out.

The Sailor in question was eventually discharged with a "less than honorable" discharge after a series of violations of military and ship regulations. Much later, his father came to the ship to plead his case. When I explained to the father what had occurred, he grudgingly admitted that the Sailor in question got what he deserved.

*****

We arrived in GTMO and were assigned to moor at a pier. The water there is azure blue and very clear. I could see the shoals near the pier. Very little wind, so I made a direct approach. We moored without incident and were boarded by the Naval Training Group Inspectors. They briefed us on the rigorous schedule for the next several weeks.

We were underway the next morning for engineering drills. For most of the day, we practiced at engineering casualty control. We were required to set GQ and Material Condition ZEBRA. Of course, we failed. An inspector found a hatch that was not properly dogged down. When we returned, I had a meeting in the wardroom to review our procedures for setting material conditions. We would do better!

Exhausting days of drills and gunnery exercises followed. There were several other ships undergoing training with us. There was a standing competition to see whose Captain could get to the Officer's Club first in the evening after the days drills.

On RICKETTS, we developed a routine that demonstrated the discipline and crispness of execution that marks a good ship. Each evening, it was a race to see which ship could get to its anchorage first. That was good for morale, racing across the blue-green sea, white water at the bow, tropic breeze fresh in your face. Of course, down in the engine rooms and boiler rooms, it wasn't quite so refreshing. Down there, the steam would drive the temperature above a hundred degrees Fahrenheit on any given day. But the Snipes loved to see their engines perform, and they could taste the cold beer waiting ashore.

As soon as the anchor was away, the pre-rigged accommodation ladder went down, the boat boom swung out and the gig was lowered. I would leave the bridge, go to the quarterdeck, embark in the gig and proceed to the club. This was a show of confidence in the Command Duty Officer and the Duty Section who remained aboard. It was also essential training in seamanship and small boat handling. We usually got to the club first. It was a welcome distraction from the grueling pace of refresher training.

*****

In mid-April, we were afforded a break in the rigorous schedule. We sailed for Ochos Rios, Jamaica for a brief liberty port.

I had seen commercials advertising the tourist trade in Jamaica, and had visions of a beautiful port with hotels and beaches. Something like Montego Bay, perhaps. I was told that we were to moor at a bauxite pier. It didn't sound promising.

We approached the north coast of the island of

Jamaica. It was about 0900 (morning). The charts were unreliable. We were at the latitude and longitude of Ochos Rios, but all I saw was jungle. I later read that the coast had been used in the 1962 James Bond film "Dr. No". It didn't look like a friendly place to take a big guided missile destroyer.

I edged my way closer until I could discern a bay. My Officer of the Deck called on the radio frequency we had been given for contact with the port authority. No answer.

I considered anchoring until I could raise someone to give me authority to enter port. No. The crew had been looking forward to a liberty port through all the hard days at GTMO. I was going to give them one! I launched the motor whaleboat and gave its crew orders to proceed into the bay, take soundings and see if they could find a pier.

My stalwart whaleboat crew motored in, pausing to take soundings and call the depth back to the watch on the bridge. The depths sounded acceptable. I edged in closer.

The motor whaleboat Coxswain called, advising that he saw a "red pier". That figured. Bauxite (an aluminum ore) can be white, gray, yellow or red. The ore in Jamaica was a reddish rust color.

I took the conn and proceeded slowly into the bay and sighted the "red" pier. It was a long wharf that ran parallel to the coast set against a lush tropic green hill. Two cranes sat idle.

As I approached the pier, my watch officer tried again to raise someone on the designated port radio circuit. Again, no answer was received. I began to wonder if somehow I had made a big mistake and was headed toward someone's pier without proper authority.

I took the ship right up against the pier, which was coated with rich reddish brown dust. Oh no, I thought. I could picture the stuff tracked all inside the ship.

I shouted down to Chief Boatswain's Mate Jerry Pugh, "Put some line handlers on the pier."

Chief Pugh nodded, pointed to several Sailors who ran to the side of the ship. I stopped the ship alongside the pier. They stepped over onto the reddish dust, received the heaving lines from the men on the foc'sle and fantail and hauled the heavy lines over, placing them around bollards.

Soon we were moored. I turned to the XO, "send an officer and two Sailors ashore to find someone, but tell them not to go much beyond the pier."

At this point, I wasn't quite sure what to expect. I felt like I was invading.

But, all was well. Soon, a sleepy looking man came out on the pier and waved to us with a big grin. Thus began our visit to Ochos Rios (Eight Rivers), a small fishing village with a bauxite mine terminal and, incidentally, no rivers. There was only a very beautiful jungle and waterfalls straight from fantasies of tropical islands. Oh yes, there was a night club hidden away in the jungle called "The Pink Flamingo." The crew got the "good time" they had worked for.

Today, Ochos Rios is a thriving tourist center and a port of call for cruise ships. But in 1975, it was a spectacular jungle hole-in-the-wall.

*****

One of the major events of refresher training was qualification in gun fire support (support of troops ashore using the ship's five inch guns). We were to fire at targets on the island of Vieques near GTMO. We drilled at the procedures over and over. As we drilled, I remembered when I first reported aboard LAWRENCE as XO. Soon after relieving my predecessor, we sailed for the Panama Canal and a Pacific transit to Vietnam. Once there, one of our main missions would be to provide gun fire support to the Marines in I Corps. I directed the gun fire support team to man up and soon discovered that they were in no way ready for the mission. So, I set up "floating island" drills most every day during the transit.

A "floating island" is simply an imaginary target in the ocean that "floats" along with you as you transit. The drills allowed the crew to get the procedures down pat. It also allowed us to shoot the guns almost every day. As a former weapons officer, I firmly believed that you had to shoot the guns as often as you could to make sure they were functioning correctly. A gun allowed to grow "too cold" is a gun that might let you down when you need it most.

*****

We arrived off the coast of Danang and were soon engaged in supporting the Marines ashore. We went to Condition II (four hours on, four hours off) and manned up all the gunnery stations with a two section watch. Day and night, we shot missions assigned to us by Marines ashore, hurling five inch high explosive projectiles at the enemy.

Captain Pete Fiedler's cabin was forward near Mount 51 and mine was aft near Mount 52. When the Captain was asleep I was on the bridge and vice versa. We normally used both gun mounts to keep the bore erosion even.

When I was in my bunk and Mount 52 was fired, the sound and shock wave from the gun would lift me out of my bunk and shake the whole cabin. But, I was so tired that I could even sleep through that, not to mention the normal rolling and sounds from the engines below.

Pete told me one night, "use Mount 52 so I can get some sleep."

So, when the mission came in, I fired it with Mount 52. Then Mount 52 had a casualty and I had to fire Mount 51.

BOOM! CRASH!

The sound powered phone squealed. A Sailor picked it up, answered and handed it to me.

"Don't tell me. Let me guess. Mount 52 is down."

"Yes Sir. Sorry about that, Captain. It should be ready to fire in about twenty minutes."

CLICK. He hung up.

After that, when it was my turn to be in my bunk, Mount 52 was fired at least once a watch. Just to get my attention, so to speak.

*****

We needed our guns one night steaming south of Danang to a new station. An urgent call for help was received on the spotter circuit. Plotting the coordinates, we found that we were close and steamed into firing position.

We put a few rounds on target and plotted some spots provided by the Marine ashore.

"Give 'em all you got".

We fired over 140 rounds, expending what was left in our magazines.

"Only illumination and practice rounds available," we reported.

"Fire those."

Our ship was credited with saving an ARVN (Army of the Republic of Vietnam) outpost from attack by a company sized unit of Viet Cong.

*****

LAWRENCE was assigned a station about thirty miles north of the DMZ (de-militarized zone) at a point where the main supply road the North Vietnamese used to move material into South Vietnam was close to the coast. With us were another destroyer and a LSD (Landing Ship Dock) that carried two Army Cobra attack helicopters. Our mission was to interdict supplies moving into South Vietnam.

We fired many indirect missions (targets we could not see) against targets identified from intelligence or air surveillance sources (truck parks, ammunition storage areas and the like). We also nailed a number of trucks coming along the road with direct fire.

We were on station for almost thirty days firing these missions, broken only by time spent to steam away from the coast, rendezvous with oilers and ammo ships and replenish. During this time, the enemy never fired back. The strain on the crew was obvious.

"Why don't they fire back?"

It was as though the crew wanted the enemy to fire back to break the boredom.

Finally, several enemy shore batteries fired back. A cheer went up from the crew. Imagine that. Happy to be shot at!

It soon became obvious why the enemy had been hesitant to fire. We plotted the position of the gun flashes quickly and put a dozen rounds on each site. Blew away the side of a mountain where they were located. Then the cobras went in and finished them off.

*****

LAWRENCE was assigned to "linebacker strike operations". These were operations above the demilitarized zone (DMZ) between North and South Vietnam. The missions against North Vietnam ranged up to and included Haiphong. We were pleased to get the assignment. To get the nod for this mission, a ship had to have two working guns and all the machinery functional to make full speed. We joined the elite.

There follows an excerpt from an article I wrote for the *Naval Institute Proceedings*.

As I finished the climb to the bridge, the thrill of danger brought a hollow feeling to my stomach. The bridge was very, very dark. As my eyes adjusted to the darkness, I stepped out on the wing of the bridge and saw that the sky was overcast with no moon. Black rain squalls moved along the horizon and lightning crackled and flashed in the distance. When it did, I could see our two companion destroyers dashing along through the choppy seas at intervals to starboard. Men began to come to the bridge to man up for General Quarters, and the subdued talk added to the ghostly atmosphere of the soft red lights in the pilot house. Silently, I walked among the men, checking the various indicators and stations. Course 335. Speed 27,

As XO, my assignment was to take the conn. The

maneuvering of the ship was mine. The Captain took station in the Combat Information Center (CIC) where he could obtain the most information to fight the ship, supervise control of weapons, and supervise the maneuvering.

"General Quarters. General Quarters. All hands man your battle stations. BONG! BONG! BONG! BONG! BONG!"

The General Quarters gong sounded loud and there was a final scurry as each man put on phones, adjusted binoculars, and arranged charts and plots into place. I relieved the conning officer and knew that 4500 tons of warship would respond to my commands. A quiet efficiency settled over the bridge. I reported to the Captain via the squawk box that all stations were manned and ready.

The radio crackled with a tactical signal that altered course 60 degrees to port and slowed the formation to 22 knots. I gave the commands and the ship leaned, then steadied and slowed. We were on a course for the mouth of Brandon Bay, right between the islands of Hon Mat and Hon Me. The approach was a controlled zig zag at varying speeds, designed to confuse enemy gunners.

I stepped out on the wing of the bridge to check my position on the guide. I could just see her outline in the gloom a mile away, but distinct and clear was the great white wave leaping at her bow. We had a "bone in our teeth" and were charging into battle.

On the horizon I could see darting, fiery tracer bullets leaping into the air after some unseen aircraft. Then more tracers. And then, the spectacular fireworks of a Surface to Air (SAM) missile launch. A great spitting ball of flame rose quickly into the air and turned in our direction. Instinctively I ducked and reached for the squawk box to warn the Captain that we had an incoming missile. It detonated before I could send the alert. A bright white flash, and seconds later, a distant KERWHUMP.

Another course and speed change. Now up to 25 knots and the wind whistled ferociously in the darkness. There was a blast of rain as we passed through a squall. We would dart like this into the firing point and turn on a course parallel to the coast to unmask all guns. After firing, we would disperse on divergent courses eastward at high speed. Normally, the coastal defense guns would not fire at us until we commenced our bombardment. That was good because it meant that most of their shells would fall behind us as we departed. Tonight would be different.

The target we were to hit was a railway storage yard. It was seven miles inland, which meant that even with the range of our guns, we had to go uncomfortably close to the beach. The Captain and the CIC team were busy pinpointing the target and inserting the track into the gunfire control equipment. They were also preparing to set up several known gun sites that were sure to fire on us.

Alter course 30 degrees to starboard. Speed 27. As the ship throbbed in response, I walked to the radar and looked into the eerie green scope. Blobs of rain squalls surrounded us. CIC was reporting many small contacts ahead. It had to be the North Vietnamese fishing fleet. Our orders were not to molest them unless fired upon, yet the maze of junks presented a considerable hazard to three destroyers trying to weave their way through them.

I saw them popping up on the scope now. Straining my eyes, I raised my binoculars and peered through the gloom and flying spray. A lookout sang out sighting a sail close on the port bow. Then I saw them in the darkness; a forest of ridged sails bobbing up and down.

Directly ahead, a series of small bright flashes stuttered. Ducking, I listened for the whine of machine gun bullets, but there were none. Raising my binoculars again, I could make out a small junk dead ahead and what appeared to be a lantern being waved frantically. I began to imagine what it must be like to be in a small boat on a dark sea and find a destroyer headed straight for you at high speed. Scary!

Several hundred yards short of the junk, I did a right standard rudder-shift your rudder-rudder amidships maneuver that took him about 10 yards down the port side. As the junk bobbed by, I looked down at the men in it and shouted at them. I don't remember what I said but it relieved my tension a bit.

Alter course 45 degrees to port. Speed 24. This was the last approach leg. The next turn would be to firing course. We had passed through the fishing fleet without incident and were in shallow water now.

"Surface search radar bearing 320." The detection report confirmed that the enemy was plotting our movements. Another search radar was detected to the southeast. "Fire control radar bearing 330." That was the clincher.

"Fire control radar is tracking."

That meant that they were on us, and I didn't have long to wait for their reaction.

Across a sector of about 45 degrees, the horizon west of us lit up with the muzzle flashes of multiple heavy guns. It was spectacular!

The next 25-30 seconds are always interesting. You know that somewhere up there, tons of lead and explosives are headed in your direction. Statistically, it's best to keep right on your course until you can see a pattern to the fall of the shot. But the urge to do something, anything, in those few seconds is overpowering.

The first salvo was a pattern of three air bursts that detonated directly ahead of the ship at a range of less than 100 yards. Everyone on the bridge ducked at the unmistakable "KERACK" of the high explosives close aboard followed by the hiss of shrapnel striking water.

The next five minutes were a blur of vivid events. Automatically, I took bearings on the muzzle flashes and passed them to the Weapons Officer. Reports flowed in to the bridge of muzzle flashes and rounds detonating close aboard. Sonar reported many close underwater detonations. Amidst this, the signal came to turn to port to the firing course and slow. With full rudder the ship swung to the new course, and as she did the two long range five inch guns swung out on the beam, tracking their target.

"KERBOOM! KERBOOM!"

The guns spoke and our bombardment went whistling on its way. Unfortunately whistles with a distinct whooshing up doppler continued, and the KERACK of incoming mingled with the KERBOOM of our outgoing. Powder fumes and cork were flying everywhere and enemy shells were exploding ahead, aft, port and starboard. Stations aft were reporting hearing shrapnel hit the superstructure.

Strangely, though you can hear it all, it's difficult to actually see an incoming detonation. You have to be looking right at it at the right split second. Tonight, though, anywhere you happened to be looking, there was a bright white and yellow flash. I was standing on the starboard bridge wing and saw one detonate abeam so close that I was looking down at it and heard the whine of shrapnel.

"KERBOOM! KERBOOM!"

Our guns kept firing. I thought to myself, will you please hurry up guns. It's time to haul out of this place. Then another spectacular sight. Deeply inland, we saw the glare of our rounds striking their target and the flare up of many secondary explosions.

WE GOT 'EM!

The squawk box came alive and a voice from CIC asked "How many rounds are we taking out there? They sound awfully close."

"Too fast, too close, too many to count," was the reply.

The guns stopped firing and the radio crackled with the dispersal signal. I put the ship into a hard port turn and cranked on 27 knots. As soon as the water got deeper, I wanted more speed and told the engineers to stand by for 29 knots.

"I can give you 32 knots and wish you'd take it," came the answer from main control.

The engineers beneath the waterline, had been getting the full effect of the numerous close aboard underwater detonations. We hauled out of there with enemy rounds chasing us all the way.

Mount 52 set up on the coastal defense guns firing at us and returned the fire. As we sped by Hon Mat Island, their guns opened up on us. We were ready for that and Mount 51 answered viciously, silencing the enemy gun. We pulled out of their gun range and escaped unscathed.

All was strangely silent as we steamed eastward, each man winding down from the tension of those few moments. It took quite a while to muster the usual wise cracks.

The next morning the crew found chunks of jagged shrapnel topside, one piece as big as a fist. We knew we had been living right that night.

*****

On another mission similar to that described in the *Proceedings* article, I had been up with XO chores for the most of the day and then to GQ at night; I was tired. We stood into another hot spot on the coast of North Vietnam in a line abreast formation of LAWRENCE, two other destroyers and a light cruiser, USS PROVIDENCE (CLG-6). PROVIDENCE had six inch guns and a TERRIER missile system. We turned to unmask our guns and began to draw fire from the shore almost immediately.

CRACKS and FLASHES all around us. Some of the explosions looked much larger than before. It was rumored that the enemy had captured some of our Army's 175 mm cannons and were using them against us.

We completed our firing mission. The signal came in over PRITAC to turn to port (LEFT) to a course that would clear the coast and increase speed. I gave the order to increase speed. To this day, I can't explain why, but I ordered RIGHT standard rudder. The helmsman put the rudder to right standard. The bow of the ship started to swing to starboard.

Force of habit saved me. As I always did, I went to the starboard wing of the bridge and focused my binoculars on the cruiser which was about three thousand yards away. All of the ships were at "darkened ship" (showing no lights) but I could see the silhouette of the cruiser clearly. Quickly, I saw my mistake and ordered "shift your rudder". Then "left full rudder". The rudder caught the swing of the ship to starboard and began to swing to port.

KERACK!

The largest shell I had seen all night detonated just off our port bow. Everyone on the bridge felt the shock wave and saw the flash. It detonated right where the ship would have been had I not given the wrong order.

The bow of the ship continued to swing to port.

KERACK.

Another shell went off, this time on our starboard bow. I ordered the helmsman to come to the new course and we outran the rounds that chased us.

I have always wondered whether the hand of "providence" guided me that night, or whether I just screwed up and caught it in time. Perhaps it was both.

Much later, long after I had retired from the Navy, I talked to a Sailor who had been aboard that night and learned that my "maneuver" had been the hot scuttlebutt topic among the crew the next day. They probably thought I was a genius or a very lucky guy.

*****

RICKETTS approached the pier at GTMO. We had failed setting material conditions again in spite of all the training and emphasis I had put on it. I was out of ideas.

As we slid next to the pier, the ship on the other side of the pier announced on its 1MC, "Fire. Fire. This is not a drill."

I turned to the OOD. "Away the Rescue and Assistance Detail." It was announced on our 1MC.

Standing on the pier waiting for the ship was the new XO, Phil Coady. It must have been a shock for him to hear all this action from his new ship. Maybe it was an omen of things to come.

As we moored, the Rescue and Assistance Detail mustered on the fantail with fire fighting equipment. As soon as the brow went over, they rushed onto the pier and to the ship that had the fire. Phil walked up the brow and reported aboard.

The fire on the other ship was quickly put out and

things returned to normal. Almost.

Phil's first exposure to his new CO was a meeting in the wardroom with all officers where I expressed my displeasure at not being able to set material conditions properly. As was my habit, I didn't scream and shout, but I'm sure it was clear to the officers that I was, at the very least, unhappy. I suggested to them that if we couldn't turn this around, I might have to take disciplinary action. I very much disliked being told every day that my ship was "unsatisfactory" in anything.

After the meeting, Dave came to my cabin with Phil in tow. "Captain, I don't think you really want to take disciplinary action on this setting material condition issue. They're doing their best. Some of these things the inspectors are finding are pretty nit picky." Phil agreed.

I absorbed this without comment. I knew they were right. The inspectors were trying to make a point about how important it was to be able to set these conditions. They were probably engaging in overkill. But, I wanted to stick to my motto of "never walk by a mistake." Maybe I had to endure the inspectors a bit longer. The morale of the wardroom was at stake, and that was more important.

"You're right," I replied. "You two get together and figure out how to pass. Attention to detail is the secret."

As they left, I told myself it was okay for the Captain to back down on some things. I made it a point to be positive and happy at the evening meal in the wardroom. By the end of refresher training we passed the material condition inspection. We achieved the highest grade in damage control during the operational readiness test recorded to that time.

*****

RICKETTS arrived back in Norfolk on 12 May, 1975. It was good to get back and have some time with our families.

Lieutenant Ben Welch reported aboard to relieve Jim Bogart as Supply Officer. As we shall see, Ben was to play a major role in the rescue of Belknap.

Now we had to face another major inspection; the Operational Propulsion Plant Examination (OPPE). We had passed the Light Off Examination. We passed GTMO. The OPPE was going to be much tougher.

*****

Chapter Six
The Mediterranean Sea

On 31 May, I took the ship to Naval Ammunition Depot, Yorktown, Virginia to load weapons. It was quite a different trip than the one to Earle, New Jersey.

We steamed up the Chesapeake Bay to the York River, along the route French ships took when they laid siege to Yorktown in the Revolutionary War. These were "home" waters to me, as in my childhood, I spent many summers with my grandparents on their farm on the York River in Gloucester County. The ammunition depot was directly across the river from my grandparent's farm. I caught many a fish in that river, sitting with my father and grandfather in an old rowboat.

As I made the approach on the pier at Yorktown, the memories flooded into my mind.

*****

My grandfather, Robert Davis Powers, had been a draftsman supervisor at the Norfolk Naval Shipyard in Portsmouth. He had worked there since he was a teenager, supporting his family after his father died. I called him "Nandy". He would sit in the bow of our fourteen foot rowboat, my father in the stern. My position was in the middle where I would row.

We would row out to the channel buoy where the "big ones" were and fish for hours. Trout, croaker and the occasional sea mullet or blue fish were the fare. Then we'd row into more shallow water and catch spot and hog fish. When we got back to the farm, Grandmother Powers would be busy frying fish. The farm house was where my grandmother grew up as Ruth Lewis. The road there is today named after my great grandfather, Joseph Lewis. I had a wonderful time on the farm with my grandparents.

I looked over at the channel buoy. Still there. Still a red conical buoy. I remembered what my father used to say when we were not getting any bites; "not holding your mouth right," he would mumble. Then he'd come out with his other wisdom about fishing: "if you're not getting any bites, you have to change the bait or move." Then we'd move, and most times start catching fish. I used his philosophy on fishing when my ship was hunting submarines. Put some "bait" out there to lure the sub skipper into going where I wanted him, then move into position to get him. It worked most of the time.

*****

RICKETTS was scheduled to deploy in July, 1975 to the SIXTH FLEET in the "Med". But first we had to pass the OPPE. There was an additional complication; the ship was not scheduled to return to Norfolk. We were to be "home ported" in Athens, Greece as part of a plan to "forward deploy"' ships. The theory was that this would save money and make it easier on the crew if they had their families with them in the Mediterranean Sea area.

The effect of the scheduled change in home port at the time was to make it all tougher. We had to prepare for a tough engineering examination and get our families ready for an unsettling move and a dramatic change in lifestyle. It was exciting to think about living in Greece, but there were many unknowns. Housing? Schools? Security? I spent a lot of time attending meetings and talking to our RICKETTS families, not to mention my own.

I was also deeply involved in preparing for the OPPE. Recently implemented, the OPPE was a critical examination of everything in the engineering department as well as a testing of the knowledge of the Officers and Petty Officers who stood engineering watches.

I had a top notch engineering officer in Steve Smith. He was more than that; he stood some of the best bridge watches as OOD. He was a leader who his men respected. Still, he would need my direct involvement.

There are two kinds of COs; those who only demand, and those who not only demand but participate. I was determined to be the latter. I spent a lot of time working with Steve and giving him all the assistance he needed. I worked to get the money he needed. I augmented his work force with others from the crew when he needed it.

*****

It was the tenth of June, 1975. Lieutenant Garry Holmstrom drove his Austin Healey 3000 to Norfolk and parked "temporarily" at the Destroyer Piers. It was late in the work day, well past lunch, so his plan was to park in the only available place, a temporary visitor parking spot, drop off his records at his new ship (RICKETTS), report aboard, then beat a hasty retreat to find a BOQ (Bachelor's Officers Quarters) room and crash for the evening.

RICKETTS was outboard a visiting Spanish Frigate so Garry saluted the Spanish flag, requested permission to cross and was halted. RICKETTS' brow had been pulled back.

"RICKETTS is getting underway for 3 days," said the Spanish Officer of the Deck.

"I'll report back later," said Garry.

On RICKETTS' bridge, Phil informed me that the new Weapons Officer was on the Spanish Frigate's quarterdeck.

"Get him before he gets away!"

The telephone on the quarterdfeck of the Spanish frigate rang. The OOD answered, listened and turned to Garry

"You are to report to the bridge of my ship," said the OOD. "I'll have you escorted there."

Garry arrived on the bridge of the Spanish frigate and looked slightly up across from their bridge wing to the widening gap of RICKETTS' bridge wing.

"Are you Mr. Holmstrom?" asked Phil.

"Yes Sir, I'll be back when the ship returns."

"Come on aboard," said Phil.

The distance between the bridge wings began to close.

"Sir, I'm parked in a temporary visitor parking place..."

"I'll take care of that."

Phil turned to a pair of strong looking Sailors. "Escort Lieutenant Holmstrom aboard!"

The Sailors extended their arms. Garry jumped. He landed on the steel deck plates and saluted.

"Lieutenant Garry Holmstrom reporting for duty, Sir."

"Any Irish blood, Mr. Holmstrom?" asked Phil.

"No Sir."

"Give us a chance!"

I issued the order, "take in all lines."

It all reminded me of when, as a brand new Ensign, I reported to Mayport, Florida and was told to board a helicopter to be transported to JONAS INGRAM. The ship was offshore conducting exercises. I got on the "flying banana" helicopter and we flew out to the ship. The crewman put the sling around my shoulders and told me to sit on a hatch in the bottom of the helicopter. The hatch was opened; I fell out (dangling on a wire). Below, on the fantail, the Sailors looked up at the green kid who was their new division officer and hauled me aboard like some "catch of the day."

Soon we were underway for the OPPE. Garry had jumped aboard with nothing but the uniform on his back.

We were underway for three days for the OPPE. The result was that RICKETTS was the first twin screw 1200 psi steam turbine ship to pass an OPPE in the Atlantic Fleet (LANTFLT) on the first try in over a year. Later, Steve saw his old CO, Captain Warren Hamm (then Chief of Staff at COMMANDER, SURFACE FORCES, ATLANTIC) and commented on that. Warren's response was something like, yes, and you guys spent more money that any DDG-2 class ship in LANTFLT.

Steve would spend all of our money, Ben would get upset, and between the two of us, we always managed to get more.

I told Garry, after we returned to port, "I have one main criteria for my Weapons Officer; when I give the order to commence firing, I want to hear some noise and see things fall out of the sky!"

Poor Garry; the fact that I had been Weapons Officer on RICKETTS put him in the hot seat. He weathered that storm and a lot more.

*****

The return to port from the OPPE trials proved to be exciting. We were once again assigned to go alongside the Spanish frigate. There was a strong current running that set RICKETTS onto the frigate. We had a pilot on board and a tug made up to our port quarter. I was happy that we had done well on the OPPE, and tired. I acquiesced to allowing the pilot to make the landing. Mistake.

The pilot misjudged the current. I could see that we were being set too hard toward the Spanish frigate so I took the conn and twisted ship against the current to lessen any impact.

SLAM.

We bumped the Spanish ship. Part of our superstructure poked a hole in the superstructure of the frigate. Visions of an international incident danced in my head. I turned to the XO.

"Get hold of Steve. Tell him to go to the frigate right now and tell 'em he and his hull techs will be over immediately to repair any damage."

"Aye aye , Sir."

Phil was off to the races.

"Hey XO,"

He stopped.

"And tell the Spanish OOD I'll be over to make my apologies at his Captain's convenience."

"Yes Sir."

Well, Steve and his Sailors repaired the damage quickly. I visited the Spanish CO. I was glad that I had studied Spanish for four years in high school and at the Naval Academy. The Captain and I hit it off, and we spent an hour polishing off a bottle of fine Spanish wine and talking in English and Spanish.

Later, we had a party with the Spanish Officers. It was a great time for all. Phil was given a tall glass of red wine by the Spanish XO and challenged to put it down. Mistake. Never challenge an Irishman to a drinking contest. Phil put the wine away and poured the Spanish XO a glass of Virginia Gentleman (bourbon). Phil put that down. It put the Spanish XO down for the night.

*****

Our hard work in the shipyard and thereafter was beginning to pay off. We began a period called "Preparation for Overseas Movement (POM) in June in which all the final details were completed and we loaded parts and stores for the trip across the Atlantic Ocean.

*****

In July 1974, the Greek junta in power in Athens sponsored a coup in Cyprus led by extremist Greek Cypriots. In response, Turkish troops took control of much of the island. Senior Greek military officers withdrew their support from the junta, which toppled.

It was decided that conditions in Greece were not conducive to home porting American ships, and our home port reverted to Norfolk.

Most of us heaved a sigh of relief. During my naval career, Phyllis and I moved thirteen times. Each time, we lost money in setting up a new home. We didn't really need the uncertainty of Athens at that time. Nor did the officers and crew.

*****

On 22 July, we held a "Dependent's Cruise", taking aboard relatives, wives and children for another cruise up the York River to the ammunition depot for our last load of ammunition before departure.

We were on the bridge, ready to get underway when the Chief Engineer called and informed me that there was a problem with one boiler (we had lit off two boilers for the cruise). Regulations said that we should have two boilers on the line when maneuvering in restricted waters (the channels of Hampton Roads and the Chesapeake

Bay).

All the dependents were aboard. It was a pleasant day for a cruise. I told the Chef Engineer to bring a second boiler on the line as quickly as possible without violating the "light-off" procedure, and to stand by to get underway on one boiler. By this time, I had enough confidence in my engineers that I could make that decision.

I always worried about having civilian dependents aboard. There are so many hazards on a ship for the uninitiated. Probably my biggest concern was the heavy water tight doors and hatches. Let a hatch swing with an unexpected roll of the ship and fingers could be missing. I told the crew that they should be with our dependents all the time. Keep an eye on them!

The cruise was fun for all, though we all knew that the day of leaving our loved ones for a six month deployment was just around the next bend. That is always a painful time for Sailors and their loved ones.

We arrived in Yorktown, put the dependents on a bus back to Norfolk, loaded our ammunition and returned to Norfolk on 24 July.

*****

On 29 July 1975, we sailed for the Med. The transit across the Atlantic Ocean was uneventful but fast paced. We trained day and night to be ready for whatever awaited us. We also had time for some fun.

When I was an Ensign aboard JONAS INGRAM, we went around the continent of Africa to "show the flag". The Captain wanted a ships' band, and I was tabbed to produce one.

And so I got the crew together, found out who played a musical instrument, and produced a six man "band". I played clarinet, saxophone and occasionally the harmonica. We played in some pretty remote places such as Mombasa Kenya and Fernando Po, a small island in the Gulf of Guinea. Perhaps the strangest place was on the Seychelles Islands in the Indian Ocean. At that time, the Seychelles were a tropical paradise with no electricity or modern conveniences.

I was also tabbed to produce a soccer team to play teams in the ports we visited. My saxophone player was also my fullback, so when we had the band play for a soccer game, it became quite confusing. To make it more difficult, this Sailor was also frequently restricted for some infraction, and I had to pledge my soul and other valuables to the XO to get him off long enough to defend the goal and play the saxophone.

So, I decided when we sailed for the Med that I was going to have a ship's band (The CVR Band). Fortunately, I had some truly talented musicians aboard. The band was led by Fire Control Technician (Missiles) Ray Jones who could sing both soul and country and western. Other members of the band were Dennis Eaves (Master of Ceremonies), Ron Morin (guitar and vocal), Jerry Potter (guitar and vocal), Tony Dela Cruz, (Bass), Bill Baker (rhythm guitar), Art Swimp (drums), and Mike Terlouw (piano, vocal and special arrangements). When they'd let me, I did a guest solo on chromatic harmonica.

Phil suffered through all this, as he was sometimes called upon to get a Sailor out of a duty so he could play in the band. He always did it with grumbling good humor, but I think he saw the value of the band as I did. At least, he said so.

The band played whenever we went alongside another ship for refueling, rearming or high line transfers. They played for ship's parties and cookouts on the fantail. They also became in high demand for concerts at orphanages in port and played at several night clubs in port calls around the Med.

This band, unlike my amateur band on JONAS INGRAM, was of professional quality. They were really good, did a lot for the morale of the crew, and made us many friends in port.

*****

We arrived in Rota, Spain on 8 August. It was a brief, busy stop as we "INCHOPPED" (reported to) to Sixth

Fleet.

We got underway from Rota and transited the Strait of Gibraltar. We were assigned to Task Group 60.1, led by the aircraft carrier KENNEDY. RICKETTS was capable of anti-air warfare (AAW, missiles and guns), antisubmarine warfare (ASW, sonar and torpedoes), anti-surface warfare (ASUW, guns and missiles), and electronic countermeasures (ECM). As such, we were one of the most capable ships assigned to protect the aircraft carrier.

Our first assignment was to play "Orange Force" (opposing force) to test the capabilities of the carrier and her air group. The Orange Force was under the command of Commodore Schultz, and RICKETTS was his flag ship (in the role of a Soviet guided missile destroyer).

I remember finding a very large Soviet satellite tracking ship and using it to screen our position from the inquiring eyes of the carrier based air group. We steamed to a position in the "radar shadow" of the big Soviet ship, between her and the carrier's estimated position. It gave us opportunity to "rig" the Soviet ship (take pictures of her for intelligence purposes and report her position). It was a lively exercise that extended for several days and provided a novel "break in" to what would be a very intense schedule.

After the Orange Force operation, we operated as a screening ship in KENNEDY's defensive perimeter as she conducted flight operations. Frequently, we were assigned to take plane guard station astern of the carrier (where BELKNAP was the night of the collision, except we were normally closer, in the fifteen hundred to two thousand yard range).

Days and nights were filled with exercises in maneuvering, communications, navigation, ASW, AAW, ASUW and ECM. Often we would be at GQ (CONDITION I) for these exercises. We continued with engineering casualty control and damage control exercises, a mainstay of our readiness to fight if called upon.

The officers stood "one in three" watches on the bridge, in CIC and in the engineering spaces. That means four hours on watch and about eight hours off, except for the "dog watches between 1600 (four o'clock PM) and 2000 (eight o'clock PM) when the watches were two hours each. This was a grueling schedule even without the exercises. But not as grueling as in the combat zone in Vietnam aboard LAWRENCE when we stood "port and starboard" (CONDITION II) watches, four hours on and four hours off.

Between watches and exercises, the officers and crew had to maintain our complex equipment and train in their job related skills. We usually ate four meals a day: breakfast, lunch, dinner and midnight rations (MIDRATS).

In overhaul, I arranged to install a ship's TV station. We ran our own entertainment system, with movies and tapes in the few hours of the day left. We also showed movies on the mess decks and in the wardroom and Chief's Quarters.

There were exciting moments in our busy schedule and few dull moments. When you're doing all these things within 5,000 tons of moving, rocking and rolling machinery filled with fuel oil and ammunition, there's no time to be bored.

*****

In August we participated in National Week Exercise in the Ionian Sea and then went to Training Anchorage in Augusta Bay, Sicily. Soon, we were off for a port visit to Taranto, a city in southern Italy. I was familiar with the name in naval history. In November 1940, the Royal Navy launched the first attack from an aircraft carrier against warships. Biplane torpedo bombers attacked the Italian battle fleet at anchor in Taranto utilizing aerial torpedoes. The damage sustained by the large Italian warships marked the beginning of the rise of the power of naval aviation (and was a forerunner to the Japanese attack on U.S. ships at Pearl Harbor).

The approach to my assigned mooring was sinuous and the charts showed the water to be barely deep enough for my ship. Once again, I sent the motor whaleboat and its crew ahead to take soundings.

RICKETTS had the advantage of two big screws, which made handling her relatively easy. The frigates had to use a tug to make a "stern in" mooring (they were single screw and had a large bulbous bow mounted sonar dome). I twisted and backed in easily.

Taranto was primarily a commercial and military port with steel and iron foundries, oil refineries, chemical works, some shipyards and food-processing factories. Not exactly a tourist mecca. You could find a place to have a beer, but that was about it for entertainment.

*****

After more Task Group Operations and plane guarding with KENNEDY, we proceeded to Naples, Italy, a more exciting liberty port for the crew.

Waiting for us were two major additions to our wardroom. Lieutenant Bill Doud reported aboard and relieved Lieutenant Mark Lodge as Operations Officer. Ensign Tim Freihofer reported aboard and relived Lieutenant Junior Grade Dave Brown as Assistant Supply and Disbursing Officer.

Naples was sort of our "home port" in the Med. It was hot, noisy and crowded, but the food was terrific and the wine and beer never ending.

Phil was an instigator of sorts, and he loved a joke. One night, he and the Department heads were having a beer at a bar near the fleet landing. Several Marines came in wearing "muscle shirts".

"Hey Marine," said Phil casually, "like to arm wrestle for a few beers?"

The Marines looked at Phil, whose physique was not of the arm wrestling type.

"Sure," said the Marines eagerly.

At that, Phil motioned to Ben. Ben came forward and put down all challengers who dared to arm wrestle. The officers of RICKETTS drank free the rest of the evening.

*****

In September, it was another training anchorage at Souda Bay, Crete and then missile and gunnery firing exercises. We did well on the live firing exercises. The discipline and training we had adopted in our weapons drills as our culture was beginning to pay off.

*****

In mid-September we steamed to Kithira Training Anchorage, an area near Greece. Frequently, we encountered Soviet warships, and we knew we'd find them at Kithira. Kithira was an unusual anchorage. It's an unprotected area in international waters with no land within sight. It is deep. Very deep. We had to "bend on" (attach) the port anchor chain to the starboard chain to make one long chain deep enough to get the anchor on bottom.

As we approached the anchorage, there were, as expected, several Soviet warships anchored there. It was a warm day, but there were no Soviet Sailors on deck. We approached cautiously, using the fathometer to find the peak at the bottom of the sea where we could set the anchor.

We anchored among the Soviet warships. We took pictures. They took pictures. This was the "front line" of the Cold War.

While we were there, helicopters brought us special visitors. First to arrive was Chief of Chaplains, Rear Admiral (later Cardinal in the Catholic Church) John O'Conner. Squadron Chaplain, Lieutenant Paul Pyrch, though at that time "riding" another ship of the squadron was aboard for the day to meet him. Next to arrive was Secretary of the Navy J. William Middendorf. He arrived in a flight suit covered with patches from ships and aircraft squadrons. We welcomed them and gave them our VIP tour.

Steve came up with the idea to write a special evaluation for Senior Chief Boiler Technician Johnny

Brown and have SECNAV sign it in order to help Johnny make Master Chief. We told all the Boiler Technicians (but not Chief Brown who was puzzled by all the intense activity) to make the after fire room look really great and we would tour Secretary Middendorf through it before asking him to sign the special evaluation.

Left to Right, Captain Powers, Honor Guard Petty Officer, Secretary Middendorf, Rear Admiral O'Connor and Commodore Schultz Aboard RICKETTS at Kithira Anchorage.

The boiler technicians loved Chief Brown and you could have eaten out of the bilges and worn sunglasses in the after fire room on the day of the visit. The Secretary signed and Johnny Brown made Master Chief on the next selection list.

Secretary Middendorf awarded the ship's engineers his "Golden Snipe" Award, recognizing the high state of engineering readiness that the ship had achieved. Commodore Schultz presented the Secretary a "Chief of Naval Operations Centurion Certificate" in honor of his one hundreth ship visit, and a miniature Surface Warfare Insignia (golden waves, the bow on image of a ship and crossed swords, referred to as "SWO Insignia", or "water wings") in remembrance of his visit.

*****

Secretary of the Navy William J. Middendorf Receives the Centurion Certificate from Commodore Milton J. Schultz. Captain Powers looks on.

*****

We anchored near Antalya, Turkey for several days, and then took part in NATO Exercise Deep Express, support of amphibious operations in northern Turkey.

Then back to Kithira where on 1 October we were visited by Commander Task Force SIXTY, Rear Admiral Carroll.

We were kept busy, moving on to escort KENNEDY in National Week XIX Exercise in the Tyrrhenian Sea. We did a lot of plane guarding.

We anchored briefly in Golfo di Castlemare and then proceeded to a port visit in Elefsis, Greece (Athens) on 14-18 October. Elefsis is where we were to be home ported had there not been a change in plans. So, the area was of more than casual interest to us.

We moored at a long pier and received a message warning us that there could be demonstrations as a result of our presence. I ordered special security set, posted sentries, checked out our emergency reaction team and laid out fully charged fire hoses.

Had there been any demonstrators or even terrorist attacks, they would have been met by armed sentries, a reaction team armed with pistols, rifles and machine guns and a hundred pounds per square inch of fire hose pressure.

Fortunately, nothing happened and we had a few beers, took in the sights of Athens and were underway to a routine repair availability in Naples.

*****

The time we spent in Naples was a special time for me. Phyllis and I had planned this for a long time. After many years as a Navy wife during deployments and my year and a half in Vietnam, she had more than earned a special trip. An art major at William and Mary, she loved all things "arty" and Italy with its rich history and many art filled galleries and churches was a special place to her.

She flew to Naples and met the ship. After we moored, I applied for some leave, told Phil to "take care of things" and rented a car. Phyllis and I were on the way to Rome.

Rome was beautiful and expensive. We tried staying in lesser hotels to save money, but after a cold night in a hotel with no hot water, I decided to live it up. And we did.

Florence was probably Phyllis' favorite. It seemed as though the list of churches she wanted to see was endless, but after a few I began to feel the sense of history and enjoyed it. More than that, I loved her and it was great to be together.

We went to various places in Northern Italy and then into Switzerland. We went over the Alps and through the tunnel at Mont Blanc (White Mountain), down to Geneva. It was a spectacular drive. Geneva is in the Rhône Valley at the southwestern corner of Lake Geneva, surrounded by mountains. The streets are cobbled with pristine parks and promenades. French influence is everywhere; iron balconies and sidewalk cafes.

We had a wonderful time. When we returned to Naples and I went back aboard ship, I felt as though I had been through some portal into a magic land and returned to reality. It was tough when Phyllis had to leave.

We sailed the day after she left for Missile and Gunnery Exercises north of Crete.

*****

By this time, the wardroom was a superbly functioning group of officers who worked and played hard. The camaraderie in the wardroom was at a peak. The Chiefs and the Officers worked well together. My confidence in my Exec, Phil Coady, was at a high. I got along well with the embarked Commodore, Milt Schultz. The hard work we had put in "getting ready" was paying off. RICKETTS was a happy ship with a proud crew. So, of course, we did well on the exercises.

Steve and the Engineers took us where we neeed to go. Bill and the Operations Department found the targets.

Garry and his Weapons Department did us proud. Things went BOOM on time and targets fell out of the sky. We had few casualties to our equipment, and the few that we had were quickly repaired as Ben and the Supply Department magically always came up with the right repair part.

*****

We returned to Augusta Bay, Sicily and anchored there during the period 17-19 November.

We got underway, rendezvoused with KENNEDY and other ships of the Task Group.

And then, it happened...

*****

Chapter Seven
First Approach

Time Magazine; As the Ricketts edged in close to play hoses on the Belknap, the destroyer suddenly found herself under fire. Three-inch shells were exploding in an ammunition locker on the Belknap, sending shrapnel whining across both decks.

I made an approach on Belknap's starboard side, my bow to her stern. The fire burned from just aft of BELKNAP's bridge to aft of her after stack.

Both of her stacks had collapsed from the collision and the fire. Burning aviation fuel and Navy distillate fuel oil put a putrid smell in the air. Black smoke roiled up from the inferno. Belknap's aluminum superstructure was melting away like a popsicle on a hot summer day.

Fire Hose Team on RICKETTS' Bow as the Ship Closes BELKNAP's Starboard Quarter
(Photograph by Dennis Eaves)

As I approached, the deck force put fenders over on the starboard side, assisted by Ben Welch. Bull fenders were toys in his arms. Hand held radios were passed to BELKNAP for bridge to bridge communications. These radios were also used to improve communications aboard BELKNAP, as fires had destroyed her normal means of internal communication.

Hose teams were formed up. All of the Officers and Chief Petty Officers were on deck, Where there was a need, someone stepped in. The XO roamed up and down the deck directing the whole operation. It was a spontaneous team effort.

Shortly after I arrived alongside, the three inch fifty caliber fixed gun ammunition stored in BELKNAP's topside ready service magazines, amidships port and starboard, began to "cook off". There were loud explosions above the roar of the fire.

POP! WHACK! BOOM! It got your attention!

The Scene From RICKETTS' Signal Bridge as Fires Rage and Ordnance Explodes on BELKNAP (Note the signal light in the foreground)
(Photograph by Dennis Eaves)

I had heard those sounds before while conducting gun strikes against coastal targets in North Vietnam while XO of LAWRENCE. I instinctively ducked.

But not for long. I was right up close to BELKNAP now, and I had placed my ship in a very dangerous position. I had to make sure we stayed close enough to the cruiser to keep the hoses on her, while not getting too close to set my ship on fire or run into her.

Fortunately, those three inch rounds were stored in a vertical position and when they went off they went straight up. Some shrapnel hit the ship, but it was spent shrapnel raining down from above.

Immediately, hose teams on RICKETTS' fo'csle, amidships and aft began to attack the fire. Some hoses were directed at the base of the fire while others were set in the spray condition and aimed high, putting a wall of mist between RICKETTS and the inferno. The fire was so intense in the amidships section of BELKNAP that her fire fighting teams couldn't reach it.

All that training and team building in the shipyard was paying off, as well as the training in GTMO. Phil and Steve moved a lot of mostly Supply Department personnel topside to the fire stations along the main deck so that we could rig more hoses. Some of the Supply Sailors rigged a fire hose on the main deck and were hanging on for dear life trying to keep it on BELKNAP while being bounced around. One of them had his eyes closed as the ammunition cooked off. But they kept the hose on the fires.

A DDG-2 class ship such as RICKETTS had six fire pumps in the engineering spaces that provided fire fighting water and also served the heads for flushing water. The engineers worked feverishly to keep all six pumps on line. Keeping the pressure above 100 psi with so many hoses spurting water and spray required their constant attention.

We had a total of twenty-two one and a half inch and two and a half inch hoses rigged. In order to maintain that many hoses, the crew has to use fire main stations inside the superstructure as well as outside, which meant rigging a number of hoses as leads from inside the ship.

As I made my approach, main control was answering the first of many bells (engine orders) that they would receive throughout the night. On a steam turbine ship such as RICKETTS, answering each bell involves controlling tons of superheated steam and feed water running through hundreds of feet of pipes on their way to the blades of the turbines that turn each shaft. Each bell puts a different demand on the boilers, which means that the number of burners feeding the fires in the boilers had to be constantly adjusted. In such a situation, the slightest error could result in a casualty to a boiler, one of the myriad pumps in the system, or to the turbines themselves.

As I maneuvered the ship, the days of casualty control drills in GTMO and elsewhere were in a corner of my mind. A casualty in the propulsion system or in the fire pumps when I had the ship in a tight spot would be disastrous. But, I had confidence in what we had done in overhaul and in the crew that we had trained. I rang up every bell I needed to keep the ship in position to fight the fires. Every order was met with a quick and professional response.

My bow was right up near the side of the big cruiser, my stern slightly away. Staying in that position (where the hoses could reach the fires on BELKNAP) in the wind and seas was tricky. I edged closer and closer. I didn't want to actually go alongside BELKNAP (close aboard, or next to her) if I could avoid it, as I knew that the ships would work in the seas and crash into each other, causing damage. Besides, the fires on Belknap were too intense at that time. The heat on my face caused me to break out in sweat.

I looked over at BELKNAP and could see melted metal from her aluminum superstructure running in steady streams along her main deck and overboard through her deck edge scuppers. Destroyers and cruisers in those days had steel hulls and aluminum superstructure (which saved weight). The fuel-fed fires were hot enough to melt aluminum! Aluminum softens at 400 degrees Fahrenheit and begins to flow at 800 degrees. I later estimated that the aluminum reached at least a temperature of 1200 degrees Fahrenheit. The metal was running freely.

I was wearing a heavy coat for a cold night. I was hot. Putting my ship alongside would have meant certain fires aboard us.

On a twin screw (propeller) ship like RICKETTS, keeping station on another ship that was dead in the water in the open sea was a matter of backing, twisting and going ahead to keep the ship in position. Using the two engines to "twist" ship aided this. This simply means opposing the engines, one ahead and one astern, to put a twisting motion on the ship that swings the bow toward or away from the nearby cruiser. I had to anticipate the movement of the two ships and order the engines and rudder to adjust for "what was coming". At the close distances involved, it required my total concentration to make fine-tuned adjustments, and a lot of bells to the engine room.

During this time Steve was quite concerned about BELKNAP's MK-46 triple torpedo tube mounts in the midships area. The three inch ordnance continued to cook off and he didn't want to take any chances with the torpedo tubes which had burning debris quite near. From RICKETTS' ASROC deck (amidships between the stacks) he stood about even with the torpedoes and they were pretty close! He had a hose team from Repair Five amidships with directions to do NOTHING but hose down the torpedo tubes all night long.

*****

In the After Fire Room, the Number 4 steam driven fire pump developed an overheated bearing on the turbine end. Boiler Technician First Class Robert Bengtson, a dedicated Sailor and engineer's engineer, personally took charge. He opened the bearing casing, removed the hot bearing halves, then blued in a new set of bearings and reassembled the unit to get it back on the line in record time. He didn't wait for it to cool down, and he blistered his hands badly in the process. This was a masterful piece of emergency marine repair, not to mention a heroic act. It was one of many such acts that night.

*****

On the foc'sle, Chief Pugh and Chief Soltes and their hose teams were at the hearth of the fiery furnace as I edged the bow closer to BELKNAP. The Sailors aimed their hoses at the base of the fire. Other hoses put up a spray to shield them from the flames.

The Sailors could see the twisted, burning metal on the cruiser. The after stack had fallen over and crushed the three inch gun mount.

BELKNAP's Starboard Side in Flames. Note the Toppled Stack at the Left Side of the Picture.
(Photograph by Dennis Eaves)

Three inch rounds continued to cook off with an occasional POP! The boat davits were a flaming mess.

Then they collapsed sending sparks flying high. It was like the collapse of a gigantic barn fire at some macabre pep rally.

"Hey, Chief. Break out some marshmallows!" Sailors can find humor in anything.

"Get that hose on those boat davits!" Chief Pugh was a no-nonsense guy.

Manning a two and a half inch fire hose under over 100 psi or more pressure is more difficult than it sounds. This is no garden hose. It's a writhing anaconda that fights whoever tries to keep it under control.

It takes several or more men to "lay out the hose", at least three men to man it and another man to "crack in" the water pressure in a way that doesn't throw the men holding the hose overboard. The nozzle man is the most important member of the hose team. He holds the heavy brass nozzle, controls the aim of the hose and operates the handle that allows water to exit the hose under high pressure. He can choose between direct stream or spray. The other two men help to lift and aim the heavy hose and back up the nozzle man.

*****

Meanwhile, amidst all this, the port side of the ship was away from BELKNAP, and that's where the davits for the motor whaleboat are located. The Commodore ordered Doctor Roger Lieberman (the Squadron Medical Officer) to go the DALE to set up an emergency treatment center. We retrieved the motor whaleboat, loaded the Doc in, and lowered away to take him to DALE. Needless to say, with everything that was going on, and with most men engaged in fighting the fire, hoisting and lowering a whaleboat while rolling in heavy seas required superb seamanship on the part of RICKETTS' Sailors.

*****

BORDELON was directed by the Commodore to close BELKNAP off the bow to 3500 yards, and then to 1000 yards to conduct boat operations to pick up survivors. Soon thereafter, BORDELON was directed to approach BELKNAP's port side to render assistance. This was the downwind side, and the flames from BELKNAP made an approach amidships impossible. BORDELON approached BELKNAP's bow and remained there about 25 minutes (without mooring), providing breathing canisters, blankets and life jackets to BELKNAP's crew. Her performance in this difficult assignment was superb.

BORDELON backed away and began to coordinate small boat operations. She transferred her hospital corpsmen to DALE and HART.

*****

As I conned the ship and the hose teams and damage control teams worked below, smoke from the fires aboard BELKNAP began to engulf the ship.

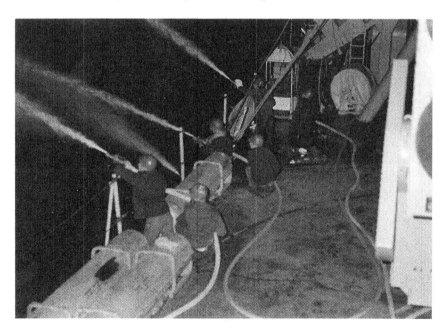

RICKETTS' Sailors Man Fire Hoses on the ASROC Missile Deck
(Photograph by Dennis Eaves)

The water from our hoses was beginning to have an affect on the fire, but the result was smoke; lots of it, thick and black. Visibility went down and soon the smoke was chokingly thick. It had a claustrophobic effect as the visibility right there on my bridge went to near zero. I had to get out of there, as I couldn't see BELKNAP, but I knew she and her fires were close aboard to starboard.

At about 2253, the sea brought RICKETTS' starboard side against the starboard side of BELKNAP. There was a scraping crunch, but the fenders rigged by the deck force took the brunt of it.

I felt a hand on my shoulder. The Commodore and I were thinking alike. I could barely see him, but as he motioned, his intent was clear. Back away.

I put the rudder over to left standard and ordered "all engines back two thirds." I had to feel my way out of there, as I couldn't see what was astern of me and I knew that other destroyers and frigates were nearby. From inside the pilot house, I heard the helmsman and lee helmsman (the Sailor that mans the engine order telegraph) repeat my orders. I heard the forced draft blowers change the pitch of their whine, so I knew the engines had answered. Other than that, I had no visual reference that we were moving away from BELKNAP. I felt the bridge bulwark to get a reference as to where I was and peered at what I thought was astern.

At about that time, the Commodore ordered me to back full. In hindsight, I now know that he was concerned that the seas were pushing RICKETTS too close to BELKNAP. I was concerned about backing into another ship.

I debated the order. Then...

"All engines back full."

The forced draft blowers whined. I could hear the noise of the fire on BELKNAP, though I couldn't see it.

I stood on the starboard wing of the bridge, felt the engines grab hold and begin backing with a powerful thrust. I peered astern through the gloom of the smoke.

A destroyer was dead astern of RICKETTS!

"All engines stop!"

I glanced ahead and to starboard. I could see the high

bow of BELKNAP and behind that the flicker of flame and a billowing cloud of black smoke. The fires were not under control, but had been beaten down.

"All engines ahead two thirds."

I had to stop RICKETTS' stern way.

I looked back and saw BORDELON about a thousand yards astern.

"All engines ahead one third."

My ship was about 500 yards off BELKNAP's starboard bow.

I watched as RICKETS lost stern way.

"All engines stop."

I was unaware of time as I assessed the situation. Damage reports flowed to the bridge; no major damage. It was, at that time, 2258 (10:58 PM) according to the ship's log. We had been close aboard BELKNAP for 38 minutes. It seemed like a lifetime. But we weren't through. The fires still burned. Her situation was critical.

I moved the ship further way from BELKNAP and stood by. We could see her better now. Her superstructure above the bridge level had been sheared off by the overhang of the carrier's angled flight deck. She had a pronounced starboard list from all the fire fighting water that had been poured on her collecting in her bilges.

*****

BELKNAP's fires were still smoldering. She was without power. She had no fire main pressure to feed her hoses.

We had to go back.

*****

Chapter Eight
Second Approach

Twice the Ricketts had to back off...

BELKNAP's crew fought valiantly, however, they were still unable to get to the fires amidships. The crew on her foc'sle were completely cut off from those on the fantail.

At 2302, I began the second approach. This time I could make a closer approach as the fires, though still burning, were not as high and the ammunition wasn't cooking off. The smoke was still thick. As we moved in, hose teams put up a wall of spray to beat back the smoke.

I came in flat and close, my bow to her stern on the starboard side. BELKNAP was rolling in the trough of the sea, wind and seas on her beam. She had no power except for an emergency diesel engine.

View From RICKETTS' Bridge (Top of Gun Mount 51 in the Foreground), Bow to the Midships Area of BELKNAP
(Photograph by Dennis Eaves)

I maneuvered to remain close alongside the burning ship, twisting, backing, going ahead; whatever was necessary to keep RICKETTS close enough to maintain our hoses on the fires.

The massive amounts of water began to extinguish her fires, and we got a closer look at the damaged cruiser. A three inch gun pointed at a crazy angle into the air.

RICKETTS' Starboard Bow Close to BELKNAP's Midship Section As Water From Hoses Beats Down the Fire. Note the Three Inch Fifty Caliber Gun Mont Barrel Pointing Upward, the Mount Completely Destroyed.
(Photograph by Dennis Eaves)

The stacks lay on top of everything, hardly recognizable; twisted masses of metal. Everything from aft of the bridge to just forward of the fantail was a blackened, sooty mess of distorted metal shapes.

As the fires midships diminished, we could see

BELKNAP's fire fighting teams working their way toward the remaining fires. Brave guys, they were determined to save their ship.

I decided it was now safe to attempt to moor to BELKNAP (tie up alongside) where we could get hoses to directly bear on the remaining flames and pass badly needed equipment over to BELKNAP's crew. I knew we would take damage from the hulls colliding in the heavy seas, but it seemed necessary.

"Stand by to moor to BELKNAP."

Over went more fenders. I worked the ship in closer until we were right alongside the high sides of the cruiser. Her topside deck was a full deck higher than mine, so mooring would be difficult.

RICKETTS' Bow Nudges Against BELKNAP'S Hull (Seen in the Background) as Fire Hoses Attack the Fires (Photograph by Dennis Eaves)

The seas slammed us into BELKNAP. This time it was a pretty good blow. Down below in the engine rooms it probably sounded like a shell hit. They were thinking, "has the Ol' Man lost his mind?" I was, at the time, thirty six years old, but all Captains are the "Ol' Man" to the crew.

I looked astern. It was clear. "All engines back two thirds." I backed away.

I backed to a position about a quarter mile on BELKNAP's starboard side and "lay to".

Meanwhile, Commodore Schultz was trying to get information from Captain Shafer on BELKNAP as to his situation. There was still a fire aboard KENNEDY, and the Commodore dispatched PHARRIS to join the carrier and render whatever assistance they could.

By 2330 (11:30 PM), RICKETTS' whaleboat and the boats from other ships had removed about sixteen wounded men from BELKNAP's stern and transported them to DALE. The Sailors in those whaleboats were true heroes, risking life and limb in heavy seas to save their shipmates. Helicopters from KENNEDY were now flying to DALE to pick up the men who were injured the worst. By midnight, twenty eight wounded men had been transferred to DALE.

Most of the injured men on the fantail of BELKNAP had been removed and taken to DALE. It was a different story on the foc'sle. BELKNAP's foc'sle was so high above a flared bow that whaleboats could not get alongside to remove the wounded. And, the men on the cruiser's foc'sle were still isolated from the after end of the ship by the fires and damage amidships.

Phil showed up on the bridge.

"Captain, I recommend we send Chief Coleman (our hospital corpsman) over to BELKNAP's foc'sle."

"Whaleboat?"

"Yes Sir. Chief says he can climb a ladder and get up there."

I hesitated. I had visions of Chief Coleman scaling a ladder under the flared bow of BELKNAP and falling into the sea. Then we'd have to deal with a "man overboard" situation." I looked over at BELKNAP and could see a group of men huddled on the foc'sle.

"Make it so."

The XO left and soon our whaleboat took Chief

Coleman under the flared bow. Men on BELKNAP lowered a rope ladder. The Chief climbed the ladder as BELKNAP rolled in the heavy seas. The whaleboat stood by, just in case.

The Chief made it to BELKNAP's foc'sle and began to administer to the wounded. I have always admired the courage of Jim Coleman for what he did that night. Brave man!

*****

Commodore Schultz was getting information from BELKNAP. Fires were still burning and BELKNAP's men were fighting them but were badly in need of additional equipment as well as medical supplies. Their fire main pressure was being maintained by one emergency diesel generator and it was dangerously low. There were eighteen badly injured men on the foc'sle. Our Chief Corpsman was the only medical assistance they had, and they were in an exposed position on a cold night. We had hand held radio communication with Chief Coleman who confirmed this.

RICKETTS had already sustained some damage. If we went alongside again, there would certainly be more. The seas had not diminished and dark clouds were covering the starlight.

Commodore Schultz made the decision.

"Bob, we have to get alongside to get the wounded men off and to DALE. What do you think?"

There was no other answer. "We can do it, Commodore."

"We have to help BELKNAP's crew fight the remaining fires midships. Can you moor to BELKNAP?"

I looked over at the stricken cruiser. Her foc'sle was somewhat higher than my 01 level (the level above the main deck). Her bow had a deep flare to it. It was not a good match.

"I'll go port to port and try to match my 01 level with their foc'sle."

Milt nodded.

I twisted ship until I got a good approach angle on BELKNAP. It was thirteen minutes after midnight when I began the third approach.

"All engines ahead one third. Rudder amidships."

A moment passed.

"All engines are ahead one third, Sir."

"Rudder is amidships, Sir."

"Very well."

That exchange of information always took place when the conning officer issued an order. It confirms that the order is understood. Then, it confirms that the engine room has answered the bell and the rudder has responded properly. There were many such exchanges that night.

RICKETTS began to glide through the swells toward the dismasted cruiser.

*****

Chapter Nine
Third Approach

With the Belknap's communications gear knocked out, Captain Walter R. Shafer had to shout commands from the bridge to his crew. Some of his men were forward, and the rest were aft around the helicopter pad. Because of the fierce blaze amidships, they were cut off from each other, and for a while the men in each group were afraid they were the sole survivors. On the forward deck, rescue crews carried wounded and burned men to a comparatively safe area in front of the missile housing, where they lay on the deck in a cold, drizzling rain.

For 2½ hours the Ricketts and Belknap fought successfully to keep the flames away from the missile housing and the ship's magazine. Chief Warrant Officer William Dockendorff, who led a team of firefighters on the Belknap, found that he had more volunteers than he could use. Tugging hoses, the men advanced on the fires, retreated momentarily when shells went off, then resumed the attack. Says one seaman who watched the battle: "That was either a bunch of brave guys or a bunch of fools."

When the fires died down, the Belknap's casualties were swung aboard the Ricketts in stretchers. Some of the men were so badly burned that they lost strips of skin during the transfer.

I passed the word down to Chief Pugh. "Shift all your fenders to port. We're going alongside."

It was eighteen minutes after midnight. I approached this time with my bow to BELKNAP'S bow. As I maneuvered alongside, it began to rain and it seemed that the wind had increased and the seas had grown higher.

Mooring to a ship at a pier is one thing; mooring to a ship that is dead in the water and moving in the open sea is quite another. I approached with a one third bell (5 knots), mentally calculating the set and drift that the seas would impose on the cruiser. I used the rudder to adjust my aim point. I needed my bow to arrive near her bow just as I adjusted to "flatten" my position alongside so as to put over lines.

"Stand by to moor to BELKNAP."

BELKNAP's Starboard Side Below the Bridge as RICKETTS Makes an Approach to Moor "Port Side To" in the Open Sea,
(Photograph by Dennis Eaves)

On the main deck, heaving lines and mooring lines were readied. The first heaving line went over at 0025 (twenty-five minutes after midnight). Sailors aboard BELKNAP grabbed the heaving lines and hauled over the larger mooring lines. Immediately, the seas picked up my ship and slammed her against BELKNAP, but the fenders absorbed most of the blow. I used the twisting motion of opposed screws to try to minimize the pounding of the two ships together. There were many more bells for the engineers to answer; no problem for my Snipes!

On deck, Phil, Steve, Greg and McClary were ready. They had brought damage control and medical equipment and had it standing by to pass to the crew of BELKNAP.

She was completely dead in the water, all boiler fires out.

Soon we were moored alongside BELKNAP. We were in the trough of the sea and both ships were rolling five to ten degrees. Occasionally, a larger swell would roll by, rolling the ships up to perhaps fifteen degrees.

This Sketch Shows RICKETTS (left) and BELKNAP (right) and How They Were Moored Together in the Open Sea. The Arrow Indicates the Position At Which BELKNAP's Wounded Sailors Were Passed to RICKETTS.

I stood on the port wing of my bridge. I looked down at the torpedo deck below me (the 01 level where the ship's torpedo tubes were mounted). When the ships leveled out, my torpedo deck was two to three feet below the raised foc'sle of BELKNAP.

Captain Shafer came to the port wing of his bridge (a level above my bridge) and looked down. He looked like he was in shock, but his square jaw was set in a determined way. He was clearly in control as much as he could be.

"What's your situation?" asked Milt over the hand held radio.

"The fires are contained to midships, as much as I can tell," responded Dick. "But we're living on one emergency generator for power."

"Have you been able to determine your casualties?"

"Not completely. I know several men in sonar control died when we collided. I've got a lot of men on the foc'sle that need to get to a hospital."

Milt looked at me. I nodded.

"We're going to get them off."

SMASH!

One of those rollers threw my ship into the side of the cruiser. I looked down. Below the bridge where I stood was the "port weather break" an aluminum shield built to keep waves from washing along the main deck as it sloped to the lower fantail. There was a big dent in the port break.

My Communications Officer, LTJG Tony Telesmanic, was on the torpedo deck below me directing men to rig wire stretchers. Although they all had their "sea legs", they had to pause as the ship rolled and hang on to the railing.

I watched the decks of the ships as we rolled. Passing men in stretchers between the two ships would be tricky, if not impossible. When one deck was up, the other was down, always, it seemed tilting at different angles. As the waves pounded, RICKETTS would bounce away from BELKNAP and the gap between the ships would widen. The heavy nylon lines with which we were moored had a "stretch factor" to make it hard to break them. So far they were holding fast, but could not maintain RICKETTS exactly alongside. In those seas, it was like being moored with giant rubber bands. Below, the bull fenders lowered to protect RICKETTS sides were being bounced and tossed around like big beach balls.

Although theoretically "moored", I used the engines to twist the ship and maintain my position with respect to BELKNAP's foc'sle as best I could. It was a "dynamic" mooring. Many more bells for my stalwart engineers were in store.

I timed the roll of the ships. As I nudged my ship

closer, every few minutes, there occurred a brief moment when the roll of the ships would synchronize and the decks were level with respect to one another.

I looked over at BELKNAP's foc'sle. Chief Coleman had the first injured man lashed into a stretcher ready to pass over. Sailors on BELKNAP tied a line to one end of the stretcher and heaved the other end over to my men aboard RICKETTS. Another line was attached to the other end of the stretcher and BELKNAP men took hold of it.

If we got the stretcher half way over and the men lost their grip, the injured man would fall into the angry seas between the ships. Lashed to the stretcher and injured, he would have no chance of survival if that occurred.

Tony was a tall, rangy basketball player, wiry and muscular. He looked up at me from the torpedo deck.

"Can you get him over, Tony?"

"Yes Sir, just get us as close as you can."

The confidence of strong youth rang in Tony's voice. He had some burly Sailors with him. They had broken down the lifelines and made a space just forward of the torpedo tubes through which they could pass a stretcher. There was a similar small space in BELKNAP's lifelines, each about four feet wide.

Over on BELKNAP, Chief Coleman gave me the "thumbs up" sign, the motion that he was ready. The expression on his face told me that the injured men badly needed medical attention.

It was a question of "feel for my ship" and timing. Music was a hobby; I knew I had a sense of rhythm. I had played center on a championship football team where the timing of the snap of the ball meant advantage to the linemen. I could do this.

I used the engines to nudge the ship forward and closer to BELKNAP' and I do mean "nudge", because if I used too much power for a second too long, the mooring lines would snap and I would have a real problem on my hands. I watched as the ships rolled; and yes, it came. That magic moment when the decks were level with respect to each other. I counted. One, two, three, four...

The decks started to move out of synchronization. That meant we had four seconds, maybe five, in which to get an injured man across the gap between the ships, above the tossing, rolling waves and the thrashing steel hulls.

Tony was watching, too. I held up four fingers. He nodded.

"We're ready, Captain."

*****

Chief Greenhouse and the cooks in the galley had been busy. The crew began passing hot bread, bologna and gallons of hot coffee and cocoa over to the crew of BELKNAP. The stream of damage control equipment and medical supplies continued.

SMASH!

The sides of the two ships came together again. I looked down from the bridge. One of our bull fenders, torn to shreds, hung by one line near the white water between the ships. Soon we would be out of fenders. Ben and Tim began organizing teams to go below, remove mattresses from the bunks and lash them together into makeshift fenders.

RICKETTS' damage control teams were busy rigging fire hoses to pass over to BELKNAP. Sailors aboard BELKNAP took the hoses and attached them to their fire main (the pipes of their fire water system). Once the hoses were attached, RICKETTS men "cut in" (opened the valves), sending water surging into BELKNAP's fire main. This allowed the men on the cruiser to better fight the fires on the other side of the ship and in compartments below.

*****

Below in the engineering spaces we were taking some damage. Steve was called down to the After Fire Room (the ship had two "fire rooms" where the boilers were installed) by Rich Celotto. The fire room crew was shoring up the hull outside the After Deaerating Feed Tank (DFT). The DFT is a large piece of machinery that removes dissolved oxygen ("air") from the condensate, preheats the feed water, and provides a storage/surge volume before the feed water is pumped into the boilers where it is turned into steam to turn the ship's turbines.

The hull was being beaten in, coming ever closer to the DFT. The DFT is a relatively thin skinned tank with a lot of water under pressure in it. If we ruptured the aft DFT, although under relatively low pressure it likely would have flashed into steam with catastrophic consequences. If that happened, we would have burned a number of our Sailors in the After Fire Room and almost certainly lost the after two boilers (two of four total boilers).

The pounding was also crushing the transverse (port to starboard) bulkheads between the Forward Fire Room and Main Engine Control, and between Main Control and the After Fire Room. These bulkheads were crushed in three or four feet and actually displaced some major steam lines a couple of feet.

Steve reported this information to me. I was most concerned about the damage to the hull near the DFT, however, I couldn't leave BELKNAP's side. She lost her emergency diesel generator and was now totally dependent on RICKETTS for fire-fighting water. Fire re-flashed up the forward superstructure burning out CIC. Her fire fighting teams needed that water badly. And, I had to get those injured men aboard and transferred to DALE.

KENNEDY's helicopters were now operating to take men from DALE to KENNEDY. KENNEDY's flight deck had become operational as her crew quickly brought the situation under control. Injured men could now be flown from KENNEDY to Naples and on to trauma hospitals in Germany.

*****

"Starboard engine ahead one third."

I nudged the bow in closer to Belknap.

"Port engine back one third."

I checked the forward motion and twisted the bow closer, watching the roll of the ships. Now, a matter of a few feet was critical. I had to match the four foot wide sections of downed lifelines of the two ships, and do it precisely at the time that both ships stopped rolling and were, for about four seconds, "in synch".

I leaned out over the bridge wing, looked down at Tony and his men on the torpedo deck.

"Get ready!"

"We're ready, Sir."

Tony motioned to Chief Coleman on BELKNAP. The Chief and his team readied the first man.

"All engines stop."

"Port engine back one third."

The ship's forward motion was checked. The bow swung in toward BELKNAP a precious few feet.

"All engines stop."

The magic moment arrived.

"Go!"

BELKNAP men thrust the stretcher out over the churning waters below. RICKETTS men hauled in on the lien attached to the stretcher.

I held my breath.

Tony, balancing precariously at the edge of the deck, reached out with long arms and grabbed one end of the stretcher. He hauled it over. Other hands grabbed the stretcher to keep the injured man's head from dropping too far as it came over RICKETTS' deck.

The stretcher was aboard!

I heaved a sigh of relief.

As each injured man came aboard, he was taken to the temporary aid station in the wardroom where Hospital Corpsman Second Class Wilson, Chief Coleman's assistant, gave them a check and prepared them to be embarked in a boat.

The injured men were in bad shape. Second and third degree burns covered their body. There were broken arms and legs. They had received morphine and had salve and temporary bandages applied to their wounds. They were still in great pain and borderline shock. Some had gone into shock. In the wardroom, the table at which we normally dined had become an operating table. The injured men were placed on it, their wounds checked and redressed and temporary splints applied where necessary.

There were two men on the ship who could get to the reserve stores of morphine; Jim Coleman and Steve Smith. Steve was the "Bulk Medicine Custodian" as a collateral duty. He was called to bring more morphine.

Later, Steve described the scene in the wardroom when he arrived as "awful." Jim Coleman had been sent to board BELKNAP, Petty Officer Wilson was in charge and Ben was his assistant. Neither Wilson nor Ben were accustomed to dealing with injuries on this scale, particularly Ben. Some of the victims were horribly burned. Those who were in the wardroom that night treating the injured deserve a lot of credit and respect; more than any award or words of praise can render,

I thought about the scene in the wardroom and what the wounded men and the men treating them were going through. I wanted to see them, reassure them; but I was glued to the bridge where my ship was still in danger.

Commodore Schultz went below to the wardroom to give encouragement to the burn victims. There's not a lot a senior officer can do in that situation but lend encouragement; and, that's very important. I had visited the wounded in hospitals with Admiral Zumwalt in Vietnam and seen how the men reacted. It's important "to care" and know that shipmates from junior to senior "care."

The second man was ready to come across to RICKETTS. My men indicated that they were ready. Their position on the torpedo deck was a precarious one. As they reached for a stretcher, they hung on to one another to keep from going overboard. Shipmates!

Again, I nudged the bow in toward BELKNAP and adjusted the fore and aft position to obtain a match at the "magic moment."

"Go!"

Another stretcher came over, was passed to waiting hands on the main deck below and taken into the wardroom.

We transferred eighteen badly injured men from BELKNAP's foc'sle in the fashion described. Miraculously, no one was injured or lost.

*****

BELKNAP was taking a pounding in the seas and listing further to starboard as fire fighting water collected in her bilges. Captain Shafer reported that he had rigged de-watering equipment (including P-250 pumps passed to him from RICKETTS) and that the ship was in no danger of sinking. Small fires and re-flashes were still being fought.

On RICKETTS' foc'sle, Chief Pugh and the deck seaman were working to keep the lines to BELKNAP adjusted and fenders (including makeshift mattress fenders) rigged. This was a dangerous endeavor, as if one of those lines parted, the end could whip around with great force, enough to kill or maim a man. Chief Pugh kept an eye on his seaman, approaching the lines only when it had to be done. Meanwhile, the fenders were continuously being ripped to shreds.

At about 0047, the number one line on RICKETTS' foc'sle parted with a SNAP. Fortunately, no one was hurt.

Chief Pugh reported that the aluminum port break had buckled inward and was essentially destroyed by the pounding against the steel hull of BELKNAP. This was not of great concern to me. It is not a structural part of the hull and is primarily intended as a shield against the weather for men on the main deck aft of the bridge.

We were, however, still being pounded against BELKNAP as the rescue operation on the foc'sle continued. I was mostly concerned about the damage to the hull that surrounded the engineering spaces. The more we pounded, the more the potential for disaster increased. All it would take was for a vicious blow to the hull to misalign a pipe or valve carrying 1200 psi steam, and men would be roasted alive in the engine rooms.

*****

I reported the damage to the Commodore. He talked to Captain Shafer on the handheld radio.

We discussed the situation.

"Captain Shafer says he needs to fight the fires on his port side where RICKETTS' hoses can't reach," said Milt. "The only way he can do that is if you keep RICKETTS alongside and hooked up to his fire main. He has no working fire pumps."

"We can do it, Commodore. But, we'll take some more damage."

"Anything critical?"

"Not yet."

"What do you think?"

I knew every minute alongside BELKNAP was a risk to my ship; and to my men. I was comfortable with the ship handling situation. I was comfortable with the way my officers, chiefs and crew was handling the siuation. What made me uncomfortable was the unknown, which was always lurking. There seemed to be no choice.

"We can stay."

The Commodore agreed that we had to remain and issued the order.

*****

By about 0200, we completed the transfer of injured personnel. We were still alongside, still pounding against the cruiser. Captain Shafer reported that the fires were out and flooding was under control

I received another report of the bulkheads in the engine rooms buckling. I was now becoming concerned about my ship. The Commodore and I discussed it. He felt I needed to keep RICKETTS alongside in case a fire re-flashed, as BELKNAP's only supply of fire-fighting water still came from RICKETTS.

At 0215, I received a report that the bulkhead at frame

83 was showing structural weakness.

SMASH!

A big wave threw RICKETTS against the side of BELKNAP. I looked up and saw the mast above the bridge shuddering as though twisted by a giant hand.

We couldn't afford a re-flash of fires on BELKNAP. Too many lives were at stake. And, a new fire could threaten the ship's magazines fore and aft. But, I had to consider my ship and my crew.

"Commodore, I suggest we break away and stand by. If there's a re-flash, I can take her back in."

Milt considered this. Every approach on a ship wallowing in the trough at sea was a risk of serious collision. Remaining alongside was a sure minor collision every few minutes.

Milt called the Captain of BELKNAP.

"Captain, we need to break away. Can you handle it now?"

Dick disappeared into his pilot house for a minute. He returned, gave Milt the thumb up signal.

"We can cope with it."

"RICKETTS will stand by in case you need further assistance."

Milt turned to me.

"Break away and stand by."

"Aye aye, Sir."

I turned to Garry. "Order the engineers to break all fire hose connections to BELKNAP. Inform all stations to standby to break away from BELKNAP.

"Aye aye, Sir."

Garry passed the word to all stations on the sound powered phones.

At 0221, all hoses were aboard.

"Take in all lines."

The deck force began to take in the lines. Number five line was stretched so tightly that it wouldn't come off the bollard. They cut it free with an ax,

"All lines clear, Captain," shouted Garry. "All clear aft."

"Very well. All engines back full. Rudder amidships."

We backed away from what had once been a proud cruiser. It was now a listing, dismasted and blackened hulk. But it was afloat.

"Left full rudder. All engines back one third."

I backed to a position astern of Belknap.

"All engines stop. Rudder amidships."

For the first time that night, I walked into the pilot house and looked at the clock. It was 0227, or almost two thirty in the morning. The pilot house crew were all at their stations as if nothing had happened.

"Mr. Holmstrom, please take the conn."

"Aye aye, Sir. This is Lieutenant Holmstrom. I have the conn."

"Also, pass the word to re-man all General Quarters stations."

"Aye aye, Captain."

The boatswain's pipe shrilled over the 1MC.

"Now re-man all general quarters stations. I say again, re-man all general quarters stations."

The crew had become scattered all over the ship performing various rescue operations. The quickest way to take muster and make sure all hands were all right was to re-man the GQ stations.

About five minutes later, the Boatswain's Mate of the Watch (BMOW) reported, "All general quarters stations manned and ready, Sir."

"Very well."

Phil came up beside me.

"XO, get a good muster and make sure everyone is okay."

"Yes sir. Doing that."

As usual, Phil was a step ahead of me.

Ensign John Pic, the Junior OOD came to me and saluted. I returned the salute. "Captain, DALE is sending their boat to remove the injured men."

"Rig the accommodation ladder, John."

The accommodation ladder is a large, stable set of steps (not actually a ladder in layman's terms) that goes over the side to receive boats. It is normally used only at anchor, but this was an unusual situation. The men we had rescued from BELKNAP's' foc'sle were badly burned, some with crushed limbs. We had to get them off the ship with the greatest of care.

"Aye aye, Sir."

"And hoist our boat aboard."

"Yes Sir."

This wasn't over. There remained a lot to do. I hadn't yet realized how tired I was. I was running on adrenalin.

I watched as Garry maneuvered the ship to make a lee on the port side (put the wind on the opposite side from that where you were going to recover the whaleboat).

DALE's boat came alongside our accommodation ladder. The seas were still running high, and the boat bobbed up and down like a cork next to the accommodation ladder platform.

"Captain," said Garry, "fantail reports we can't get the injured personnel in DALE's boat. Request permission to lower our boat again and bring DALE's boat to the rails. I think that'll work."

"Make it so."

*****

Milt was in CIC, and he was busy. He had a lot to think about; a whole squadron. Later, when I was a squadron commander, I thought back to that night and went through the mental drill of "what would I have done?" And "how many things there were to think of!" You had to stay constantly ahead of what was occurring, think of what had to be done next, prioritize your actions, and above all, do what needed to be done to head off any further disaster. Not easy. From where I stood, Milt was doing a great job.

The report came in from BELKNAP that she was structurally sound and ready for towing. Milt directed BORDELON to prepare to tow BELKNAP to Augusta Bay, Sicily.

*****

I stayed on the bridge. We hoisted DALE's motor whaleboat to the rails on the main deck and loaded the injured men directly into it. All of the injured men were on their way to DALE by 0335. All total, about seventy five men had been evacuated from BELKNAP. Captain Shafer reported that the remaining crew were well. They wanted to stick by their ship, and would remain aboard while under tow. Initial reports indicated that there had been six fatalities aboard BELKNAP. It was the next morning before the accounting of BELKNAP's crew was completed..

*****

At about 0458, BELKNAP reported a fire had re-flashed between the 01 and 02 level starboard side midships. She reported that she had no fire main pressure.

I was up from the Captain's chair and on to the starboard wing of the bridge. I expected we would be told to go alongside again. Instead, the Commodore assigned BORDELON to assist. BORDELON went in and directed fire hoses at the re-flash. As usual, BORDELON did a superb job.

At 0521, BELKNAP reported a re-flash of a fires; one on her signal bridge and another behind where the after stack used to be. The crews of BELKNAP and BORDELON fought the reflashing fires. At 0532, BELKNAP reported that she had one fire pump working and was able to handle the fires.

BORDELON backed away and prepared to take the cruiser under tow. All destroyers and frigates carry a "towing hawser" and are trained to tow another ship. The need to perform this task could occur in battle or in any rescue at sea situation. Aboard LAWRENCE, when we steamed into enemy waters to fire at shore targets, we rigged the towing hawser in case we had to tow a fellow ship out of harm's way. We also laid out lines so that we could perform an emergency tow; that is, a mooring alongside (much as we actually did with BELKNAP) to pull a damaged ship out of harm's way. This method was to be used if the ships were under fire and lacked time to rig the towing hawser (a more lengthy operation). BORDELON would employ the towing hawser to tow BELKNAP.

*****

As dawn broke, we got our first daylight glimpse of BELKNAP. It was a depressing sight. In her prime, she had been a beautiful and proud warship with the latest technology. Now, after a series of disastrous mistakes she was a dismasted, blackened wreck, her decks a mass of twisted metal.

BELKNAP's crew had performed heroically in the worst of circumstances. They still had their pride, even though hearts were broken over the loss of shipmates. One had the feeling, however, that BELKNAP would live again to serve her country.

*****

Chapter Ten
Aftermath

At daybreak the Belknap was a smoldering hulk in the water, her superstructure a jumble of twisted steel and aluminum; the damage was so extensive that she may have to be scrapped. The Kennedy, which had quickly extinguished her fire, suffered only minor damage to her flight deck and soon was again launching planes. One man was killed on the Kennedy, and six on the Belknap. Forty-seven members of the Belknap's crew were injured, 21 severely. Casualties would have been far higher if the crews of the Belknap and the Ricketts had not fought so heroically through the night.

Somewhere around dawn, BORDELON took BELKNAP under tow. Lieutenant Junior Grade Wayne Rowe assumed duty as officer of the deck.

BELKNAP under tow by BORDELON
(Photograph by Dennis Eaves)

The squadron proceeded to do a "close area search" of the entire area, calculating the direction of drift from the point of collision. We were still searching for men in the water, because, at that time, BELKNAP could not ascertain total accountability of her crew. The accountability remained an issue for the next day. Finally, we were able to establish that no Sailor had gone overboard,

I remember addressing the crew on the 1MC. I can't remember what I said, but it went something like this; "This is the Captain speaking. I'm very, very proud of the way in which all of you performed, supporting the ship, me and each other in a time of peril and tragedy. You lived up to the name "shipmate" in every way. Thank you. Please take a moment in your prayers to remember those who were killed or injured. That is all."

For the first time in almost twelve hours, I went below.

I had a light breakfast in the wardroom, but I had no appetite. I went to my cabin; lay down and tried to rest. It was no use. I had been on an adrenaline high for so long, it would take a quite a while to return to normal sleep patterns. I laid there, wide eyed, and thought about what had just happened.

My first thought was about the men who had died. I had seen death before in Vietnam. I had suffered through the death of men I knew and respected. But here, in the Ionian Sea, on a routine night exercise, no one could have suspected that death was lurking. It brought home to me the reality of life aboard destroyers; racing through seas in a metal hull full of fuel and ammunition, at night, in the day, with other ships or even without them, in fair or foul weather, against an enemy or in relative peace, death was always lurking. Yet, I loved it. The excitement of it. The camaraderie of standing into danger with my shipmates. I understood the responsibilities of command better than ever before and resolved to never, ever, allow myself to put my men in danger that could be avoided. I recognized, however, that a warship is designed to "go in harm's way" and that I would face more situations where I had no choice but to go there.

My second thought was of Captain Shafer. He had lived through an event that would tear at his soul the rest of his life. I tried to imagine what he must feel like, but couldn't. It was unimaginable. Tragic.

My third thought was about my men aboard RICKETTS; the pride I felt in the way they had performed under a great deal of pressure in a very dangerous and life threatening situation. There were many, many heroes that night.

My fourth thought was about the families of men aboard BELKNAP, KENNEDY, RICKETTS and the other ships of the Task Force. When their loved one sailed off on a ship, to be away for at least six months, there was always a sense of loss; of time together, of shared joys. There was also the expectation that he will come back, even when combat is involved. Some of KENNEDY's and BELKNAP's men would not be going home.

I called Phil and asked him to send off a telegram to Phyllis and the ship's Ombudsman (a Navy wife designated to liaison with the ship for information and "take care" of the families while we were away), telling them that all the men were alright and not to worry about what they might read in the news.

My last thought was about fate and luck. As the saying goes, "there but for the grace of God go I." I was fortunate that RICKETTS had not been not in a major collision, though I like to think that my vigilance and that of my crew had something to do with that. I was fortunate that I did not make a fatal error in the way I handled the ship. I was fortunate that there were no casualties in my crew. I was fortunate that the bulkheads didn't crumble, and that the steam pipes didn't burst. I was just plain lucky. I also knew with some satisfaction that in many ways, you make your own luck in the way you prepare to do your job and anticipate the best and worst of circumstances.

My ship had been ready.

*****

I went back to the bridge. The ship was patrolling the area, conducting search and rescue (SAR) operations.

Steve came to the bridge. "Captain, we have damage at frames 83 to 110, starboard side and some damage to the port side in the engine rooms. I've looked at it. My Chiefs have looked at it. We don't consider it to be serious, though it will have to be eventually repaired."

"Question is, is it mission limiting? Can we complete the deployment?"

"In my opinion, it isn't. We'll have to see what the NAVSEA (Naval Sea Systems Command) guys say in Naples."

I informed Commodore Schultz of our evaluation and told him I saw no reason why we could not complete the deployment.

As it turned out, no one went into the water that night. Late in the evening we terminated the SAR operations and took a course toward Augusta Bay, Sicily.

*****

I was in my cabin. I had finally gotten to sleep; it was the deepest sleep I've ever had. Once sleep overtook me, my body recognized my fatigue and I was "out".

The shrill sound of the sound powered phone tried to awake me. I rolled over, fumbled for the phone, picked it up and put it to my ear, still in bed.

"Captain here."

This was not unusual. As Commanding Officer, my officers were required to call me if ever in doubt about the situation on the bridge, in the ship or what was going on around us. Captains get used to sleeping in one to two hour segments when at sea.

Steve was on the phone. "Captain, we're nearing Augusta Bay and there must be a hundred or more "skunks" (the name for a radar contact or ship in the vicinity) out here. I think you'd better come to the bridge."

Fatigue was my companion as I responded, "You can handle it, Steve." I knew he could. I also knew he was right.

"I'd feel a lot better if you'd come up here, Captain."

"Okay, Steve. I'll be there."

I crawled out of bed, stepped into my khakis and climbed up the one level between my cabin and the pilot house. The Pilot house was dark.

"Captain's on the bridge," announced the BMOW.

Steve came to me and saluted. I returned the salute. He gave me all the current information; our course, speed, where the other ships of the force were, etc. As I listened, my eyes adjusted to the darkness and I could see lights all around us; ships, boats, lots of them. I thought about that terrifying moment when Captain Shafer had burst onto his bridge and been confronted with impending death. I shook it off.

I walked to the radar scope and peered into the rubber hood that covered it. The radra scope looked like a kid with freckles; contacts everywhere. I watched the screen for about a minute, taking in the relative motion of them all.

"Skunk Sierra bears 020 degrees true at a distance of 9,000 yards, is closing and has a CPA of 030 degrees relative at a distance of 4,000 yards," announced the bridge phone talker, relaying information from CIC.

"Very well," responded Steve.

I walked to the Captain's chair, climbed into it, leaned back and watched.

"Left standard rudder," ordered Steve, "come to course 060."

"Left standard rudder," responded the helmsman, "come to course 060."

Steve glanced at me. I said nothing; closed my eyes. He knew what he was doing. It helped him that I was there. And I felt better now that I was. Occasionally, I would get up, walk to a bridge wing, look around, assess the situation, look at the radar scope and go back to my chair.

Steve was an exceptional officer. If the Officer of the Deck aboard BELKNAP had been fully qualified, he would have demanded Captain Shafer's presence on the bridge as soon as he felt he was "losing the picture". Steve did it even when he "had the picture", just because it was a stressful situation and he felt I should be there.

*****

We anchored in Augusta Bay on November 24. Nearby, BELKNAP was anchored. I stood on my bridge a long time after the hook went down and looked at her. I re-lived the collision, the rescue, the whole thing.

Aboard the BELKNAP, the investigation had already started. An inspection team was aboard to survey the damage and began the questioning of her officers and men.

Soon, the investigating officer boarded RICKETTS and inspected the damage to the ship. The port break was warped and bent and would have to be replaced. But, it was still functional. There was also significant damage to the starboard break. Frames in the fire rooms and engine rooms were buckles in a few feet.

*****

Four days later, we moored once again in Naples. It seemed just yesterday that I had said goodbye to Phyllis here. We were back.

As BELKNAP was towed into the harbor, USS PIEDMONT (AD-17), a destroyer tender veteran of World War II, the Korean War and Vietnam, then stationed in Naples to service destroyers of the SIXTH FLEET, rendered "passing honors" to her. PIEDMONT sounded "attention on deck" and all Sailors aboard saluted. This ceremony is carried out when two ships pass close aboard in port or in special ceremonies, the junior ship rendering honors to the senior. In this case, it was clear that PIEDMONT was honoring the brave Sailors of BELKNAP. It was a touching moment.

*****

I was asked to attend a press conference. I did, and related as briefly as I could what had happened, the role of my ship, and the heroic actions of my crew. Phil kidded me later that I had begun "It was a dark and stormy night; a favorite line of Snoopy in the "Peanuts" cartoon when he was playing the "Red Baron". Well, it WAS a dark and stormy night.

My favorite quote that came out of the various news conferences was made by one of my senior engineers to the effect, "The Ol' Man took us in there, and we had to get him out."

*****

We received a lot of praise for our rescue and assistance mission. Some of the messages received:

From: Commander Task Force Sixty
Addressed to Task Force Sixty

The tragic events of last night are still not close to being fully understood or accepted. We all share the shock and sorrow or the loss of shipmates and for the pain and suffering of many others. As professionals we are hurt by the sense of failure that always follows an accident at sea.
Yet in spite of all the hurt we feel, we also sense the true spirit of the Navy team which always reaches its peak in moments of great peril and challenge. The many individuals who form the Task Force Sixty Team reached those heights last night. Heroism was the common standard and selfless service to ship and shipmate was the order of the day.
Of course, USS JOHN F. KENNEDY and USS BELKNAP bore the brunt of the challenge and hundreds of individuals in those ships performed with skill, determination and valor.
USS C.V. RICKETTS was operated by fearless Navy men who came alongside the fiercely burning and exploding BELKNAP to rescue trapped men and fight the holocaust.
T.C. HART, PHARRIS, BORDELON and DALE were all active in rescuing and caring for injured men as well as fighting fires.
Our ships were joined by helicopters flown aggressively by the air crews of HS-11 and HSL-3 in the search for survivors and to medevac shipmates.
The Navy is made up of countless individuals who join

together in common purpose. Last night each one of you was outstanding. Together you made an unbeatable Navy team. I am proud to be a member of that Navy team with each one of you.
RADM Carroll.

*****

From: Commander in Chief U.S. Naval Forces Europe
Addressed to all ships of the Task Group.

Traditionally our strength in the Navy has been the ability to perform in the face of adversity. You are without doubt reaffirming that proud tradition. I have been watching with pride and admiration the superb individual and team reactions which have been directly responsible for gaining rapid control of the conflagration. Well done. Admiral David H. Bagley.

*****

From: Commanding Officer, USS BORDELON
Addressed to USS CLAUDE V. RICKETTS

Performance by RICKETTS in assisting BELKNAP made us proud to be in the same Navy with you. Fantastic.

*****

Commander, SIXTH FLEET
Addressed to Ships and Units of the Task Group

As you are well aware, USS JOHN F. KENNEDY and USS BELKNAP were involved in a collision at sea during the night of 22 November. Subsequently, each of you played a significant part in the search and rescue operations which lessened the loss of life and minimized the impact on fleet readiness. Effective damage control, quick assistance, efficient search activity, early evacuation *of the injured, sound seamanship, and obvious leadership and coordination were widely evident. No fleet commander could ask for more.*

I'm sure that many individuals will be singled out in the days ahead, as they properly should be, for exemplary conduct. In the interim, I would like to pass along to each of your commands and to you, the commanders, my greatest admiration for your professionalism and for your care and concern of all naval personnel involved.
Vice Admiral F.C. Turner, USN

*****

From: Commander Naval Surface Forces, U.S. Atlantic Fleet
Addressed to USS CLAUDE V. RICKETTS

The performance of the officers and men in USS CLAUDE V. RICKETTS in rendering assistance to BELKNAP in her hour of need should be a source of pride to all. You recognized and responded immediately to BELKNAP's need under what can only be described as very difficult and trying circumstances, thus demonstrating a readiness posture and unselfish devotion to duty of the highest order. Well done.
Vice Admiral Adamson

*****

From: USS BELKNAP
Addressed to ships and units of the Task Group

You have won the everlasting admiration and gratitude of the men of BELKNAP. Your heroic and unselfish actions and outstanding professional abilities in our hour of tragedy were a major factor in the survival of BELKNAP and her crew. Thank you and God bless you.

*****

These were all great "kudos". But I understood that an investigation was a different matter. Navy engineers were on the way to inspect the damage to my ship.

*****

Chapter Eleven
The Investigation

There were starkly conflicting versions of the courses steered by the Kennedy and the Belknap, leading to the disaster that all Sailors fear — a collision at sea. The Navy began an investigation to determine who or what was at fault when the carrier and the cruiser started a maneuver that should have been so simple but ended so tragically.

Nothing at sea in a night formation is simple, though to a landlubber looking at it on paper, it may seem so. You don't know the meaning of dark and confusing until you've been on a Navy ship's bridge while the ship is maneuvering in formation at night. Everything looks different. It takes knowledge and steel discipline to keep the situation under control; things that were lacking that night aboard BELKNAP and JOHN F. KENNEDY.

These thoughts were on my mind as RICKETTS returned to Naples and moored in the harbor. It was 29 November, 1975. The investigation was beginning, and I was to report immediately.

In my mind, I had done the right thing. The actions of my crew had saved lives. Still, my ship had been damaged. Inspectors were due aboard in the morning to determine the extent of the damage. I was accountable. I prepared myself for what I imagined would be an ordeal.

I thought about Commodore Schultz. His orders to the squadron had resulted in a well-coordinated search and rescue operation. My crew in CIC and radio had been a part of that, as had Bill Doud. The Commodore, too, was accountable. We did not discuss what we would say at the hearing. I was confident that I would have his full support.

*****

I found out later that Captain Gureck had been relieved of command of KENNEDY that same day by

Captain John R.C. Mitchell. It was a normal change of command, as far as I know. I did not receive an invitation to a change of command ceremony, so I assume it was a hurried affair with minimum ceremony.

I took one of KENNEDY's boats to board her at anchorage. In the boat, I felt all eyes on me. It was an uneasy feeling.

Climbing aboard reminded me once again how immense aircraft carriers are. It would take over fifteen of my ship to even come close to equaling the tonnage.

*****

I had heard all of my naval career that you don't want to have to sit at the long green table. In the hearing room, there was indeed a "long green table" (a long table covered with a green felt-like material). Here I was.

There were a lot of Captains and Commanders in the room. I assumed that many of them were Judge Advocate General (JAG) officers, or Navy Lawyers. I was also sure that they all knew my father. They were probably Lieutenants when he had been a Rear Admiral in JAG. I didn't know if they knew of the relationship; not that it would have made any difference.

My father used to say that there were two kinds of JAG officers: the kind that told the line officers (those eligible for command at sea) what they couldn't do, and those who told the line officers how to legally do what they must do. He was one of the latter. He demonstrated that when, during the Cuban Missile crisis of 1962, a naval "blockade" of Cuba seemed a viable option for President Kennedy. But, a naval blockade is, under international law, an "act of war". The President did not want to provoke Premier Krushchev and the Soviet Union; he wanted to get the offensive missiles out of Cuba. So, Dad, in the Pentagon with Navy JAG at the time, defined a new set of rules and called it a "Naval Quarantine," defined to be an act short of a declaration of war, but establishing an area where certain types of weapons would not be allowed. Words are important.

I wondered which kind of lawyers these officers were.

*****

I was escorted to a waiting room where I cooled my heels. I had no legal counsel. I was on my own, which didn't bother me. Command is often lonely. Finally, my turn came. I went into the room with the long green table.

The room was filled with officers standing around talking. I was surprised to see Bill Gureck there wearing the two stars of a Rear Admiral. He seemed calm and jovial and was chatting with several other officers. Captain Shafer was there; quiet, dignified, obviously engaged in "stiff upper lip" control.

The investigation had been directed by Admiral David Bagley, Commander in Chief, U.S. Naval Forces, Europe. The tasking to the investigating officer said, in part: *"The investigation is directed to inquire into all the facts and circumstances connected with the collision; the damage resulting therefrom including damage incurred to other vessels rendering assistance, particularly USS CLAUDE V. RICKETTS (DDG-5); and death and injuries to naval personnel, as appropriate, to perform the duties of an inquest; and to fix individual responsibilities for the incident."*

The preliminary statement of the Investigating Officer (Rear Admiral Donald D. Engen, a naval aviator) stated that *upon completion of a preliminary inspection, he concluded that there was no evidence of material or equipment failure as a cause of the collision.* He also concluded that *the conduct or performance of one or more of the Commanding Officers or Officers of the Deck of the two ships might well have contributed as a cause of the collision and thus be subject to inquiry. The decision was therefore made to designate the two officers in each ship parties (a party is a person subject to inquiry)." Captain Walter R. Shafer, U.S. Navy, Commanding Officer, USS BELKNAP, and Lieutenant Junior Grade Kenneth Knull, U.S. Navy, Officer of the Deck of USS BELKNAP at the time of the collision were informed of their designation as parties.*

The Preliminary Statement went on to say that *the designation of Captain (Now Rear Admiral) Gureck and Lieutenant Commander Vester (KENNEDY's OOD) as parties was withdrawn prior to the adjournment for deliberations, their conduct or performance of duty no longer being subject to inquiry.*

No reason was given as to why the performance of duty of Rear Admiral Gureck and Lieutenant Commander Vester was no longer subject to inquiry.

*****

The questions asked me were routinely brief. I was asked to describe what had occurred. I did so as briefly as possible.

Then I was asked, "Captain Powers, did you hazard your ship?"

This was a loaded question. Article 110 in the Uniform Code of Military Justice (UCMJ) is titled "Improper Hazarding of Vessel." In essence, it says that *any person subject to this chapter who negligently hazards or suffers to be hazarded any vessel of the armed forces shall be punished as a court-martial may direct. Elements of this offense are that a vessel of the armed forces was hazarded in a certain manner and that the accused by certain acts or omissions, willfully and wrongfully, or negligently, caused or suffered the vessel to be hazarded.*

I was well aware of this article in UCMJ.

"Yes Sir, I did. I had no choice."

There was a rustle in the room, a pause, and the senior officer called for a break. As I got up to leave, I heard one of the JAG officers say to another, "no wonder he's well spoken. That's Bob Powers' son."

I had a brief moment of pride. But I knew I was just as accountable for my actions as any other Captain. As it turned out, I was not called back to testify. The recommendations of the investigating officer followed the recommendation sent by Rear Admiral Carroll, as follows: From: Commander, Task Force Sixty

Addressed to Commander, Sixth Fleet

Based on my personal observation the actions C.O. USS CLAUDE V. RICKETTS carried out under the conditions described in reference A (a separate message), reflect the highest standards of courage, professionalism and seamanship.

I fully concur with the decisions of Commander, Destroyer Squadron TWENTY TWO and C.O. RICKETTS that the BELKNAP and her crew might not have survived the holocaust which engulfed her without the immediate and direct assistance provided by RICKETTS.

The damage sustained by RICKETTS during the rescue and assistance operations the night of 22/23 November is judged to have been received as a direct result of essential military operations and in no way should reflect unfavorably on the judgment and performance of Commander, Destroyer Squadron TWENTY TWO and C.O. USS CLAUDE V. RICKETTS.

Commander Destroyer Squadron TWENTY TWO, his staff and the officers and men of USS CLAUDE V. RICKETTS have my highest admiration for their performance during the rescue and assistance operations.

*****

At the informal investigation, Commodore Schultz testified as to why the collision occurred. He vouched for the fact that the CO's place is on the Bridge in major evolutions (i.e. beginning & recovery of flight operations, or any other major evolution). He observed that collisions or other casualties happen during the completion of one exercise and before the next scheduled one when watches are being relieved, changes in conditions are set and there is no one (except the Commanding Officer) who holds the bridge together, calmly, positively, and quietly.

The Commodore observed that "one's time in command is so precious an opportunity that one should not waste it by not being present on the bridge for major evolutions of any kind. I had four commands and used the above procedures to keep me out of trouble."

*****

This investigation, in 1975, occurred eight years after the sinking of the Israeli destroyer EILAT by an Egyptian Soviet-built *Komar* class missile patrol boat. The patrol boat fired four *SS-N-2 Styx* missiles at EILAT on October 20, 1967, shortly after the Six Day War, causing it to sink with a loss of forty-seven men.

A debate had raged in the U.S. Navy for all those eight years over the vulnerabilities of U.S. aircraft carriers to such an attack. In 1968, while Weapons Officer of RICKETTS, I participated in a study to determine the best defense against cruise missiles. There were few options at the time.

When the collision between BELKNAP and KENNEDY occurred, there was a high sensitivity among the naval aviation people regarding how much damage a carrier could sustain and keep operating. No doubt, the last thing they wanted was an incident that highlighted the vulnerability of a carrier.

Fortunately, the damage to the carrier in this case was not serious and her crew reacted heroically in putting out the fires and restoring the flight deck to a "ready" status within a few hours of the collision.

This debate rages on unabated as carriers have grown in size and missile technology has improved and spread to other nations, including potential enemies.

*****

The "findings of fact" in the investigation were long and written in Navy legalese. In the following chapters, I summarize the findings and explain them in layman's terms.

*****

Chapter Twelve
On KENNEDY's Bridge

At 1800 (6:00 PM), the OOD was Lieutenant Commander D.B. Jessel. The officers on the bridge were busy preparing for flight operations.

Commodore Schultz assigned PHARRIS as "plane guard" for KENNEDY flight operations. At about 1845, KENNEDY contacted the Commodore's staff watch officer and informed him that KENNEDY's TACAN was "down." PHARRIS' TACAN was also down. KENNEDY asked which ships had a functional TACAN. The Commodore was notified of the discussion. A quick check indicated that the only ship available at the time with a functioning TACAN was BELKNAP. KENNEDY was so informed.

KENNEDY dismissed PHARRIS and "took" BELKNAP as plane guard. KENNEDY did this without consulting further with Commodore Schultz.

Plane guard duty was not normally assigned to cruisers. They were not experienced in the assignment. Being larger, the cruisers are also not as maneuverable as destroyers and frigates. The Commodore would have preferred to assign one of the destroyers or frigates as plane guard.

If BELKNAP had remained in the screen with the other cruisers, destroyers and frigates, she would have been only three to four miles from KENNEDY. By putting BELKNAP in plane guard station at a distance of 4,000 yards behind the carrier, KENNEDY gained only two miles with regard to TACAN positioning.

It was a stormy night, however, the visibility was ten miles according to the hearing report. We could clearly see the carrier from our station in the screen, three to four miles away. The hearing report states that the cloud cover was scattered and broken and ranged from 2,000 to 7,000 feet. A returning aircraft homing on BELKNAP's TACAN could, once the formation was in sight, easily distinguish between the cruiser and the carrier, even if the cruiser had been three to four miles away instead of two. However, at the time, the perceived need for a TACAN ship near the carrier drove the decision.

*****

The wind was from the northeast, so KENNEDY would turn to the northeast to recover and launch aircraft (into the wind), and when that operation was complete, turn down wind to the southwest (so as to remain within her designated operating area).

KENNEDY assigned BELKNAP's station as starboard 170 degrees relative to KENNEDY at a distance of 4000 yards (behind KENNEDY and 10 degrees to the right of her wake).

As BELKNAP took station, KENNEDY was on flight course (optimum course to launch and recover aircraft) of 020 degrees.

BELKNAP took the designated station without difficulty. KENNEDY completed flight operations (launch and recovery of aircraft) at 1916 (7:16 PM). The OOD, Lieutenant Commander Jessel, cleared his plans with Captain Gureck (who was on the bridge at that time) and directed the Junior Officer of the Deck for Communications (JOOWC) to send a signal that would reverse course to a downwind course. A carrier has an officer on the bridge whose primary duty is to code, prepare and send signals, as well as receive signals. The signal was "executed" (directed to take place) at 1918. KENNEDY turned to port (left). BELKNAP, from her position slightly to the right of the carrier's wake, fell in behind and followed the big ship around to the new course.

BELKNAP's station was then changed to port 150 at a distance of 4000 yards (behind KENNEDY and 30 degrees to the left of her wake). The reason provided for this change was that it was easier for KENNEDY to see to port from her bridge (looking out across the flight deck). Soon thereafter, the station was changed to port 160 at a distance of 4000 yards (ten degrees closer to the carrier's wake).

Plane guard station is usually 15-20 degrees to port

(left) of the carrier's wake to allow for the nine degree angle to port of the flight deck. If stationed to starboard of the wake, the aircraft would be coming in for landing nearly directly over the plane guard ship. At 4000 yards, that doesn't make much difference. Closer, it does, as you don't want the pilots worrying about clipping the plane guard's mast.

During the period 1845 (6:45 PM) and 2115 (9:15 PM), KENNEDY executed several turns with BELKNAP maintaining her position relative to the carrier ("relative" means that BELKNAP's station remained astern of the carrier at 4000 yards no matter which way the carrier turned or what course the carrier was on. BELKNAP was ordered to essentially follow the carrier just to the left of the carrier's wake).

At 2000 (8:00 PM), Lieutenant Commander James A Vester relieved as Officer of the Deck. Lieutenant Richard L. Podorsky assumed duties as Junior Officer of the Deck. Lieutenant Podorsky assumed the "conn" (control of ship's rudder and engines), under the supervision of Lieutenant Commander Vester. Lieutenant Podorsky had the conn until Captain Gureck took the conn about three minutes before the collision.

At 2001 (8:01 PM), KENNEDY turned to starboard (right) to the northeast to launch aircraft (up wind). At 2115 (8:15 PM), she executed a turn to starboard (right) to the southwest (downwind).

BELKNAP executed the turns that took place between 2000 and 2115 successfully. Both of these turns were to starboard (right), a turn away from BELKNAP's position to port of the carrier's wake.

At 2130 (9:30 PM), the carrier was on course 200 degrees (roughly southwest) at a speed of ten knots.

At 2144, while in his sea cabin (a cabin near the bridge) Captain Gureck approved the OOD's request to transmit an order to turn to port (left) to course 025 (roughly northeast) and increase speed to 12 knots to recover aircraft. This was a turn to the left of 175 degrees, five degrees less than a full course reversal. It was also a turn in a direction different from the previous two turns (left vice right).

This was not unusual, as it is normal to turn in the direction that involves the least change in course (if she had turned to starboard, it would have been a course change of 185 degrees, or five degrees more than a full course reversal).

However, it was a turn in the direction of BELKNAP's station 20 degrees to the left of KENNEDY's wake. This meant that if BELKNAP, for any reason, failed to get astern of the carrier and "follow her around", remaining near her wake, KENNEDY would be headed almost directly at BELKNAP upon completion of her turn.

At 2152 (9:52 PM), Captain Gureck came to the bridge. As the carrier turned to port, KENNEDY's OOD alerted Captain Gureck regarding his concern for BELKNAP's movements. She had not remained in the carrier's wake, but was on the port beam of the turning carrier.

At 2155, KENNEDY's conning officer (the JOOD) eased his rudder to left ten degrees to slow the turn of the carrier.

BELKNAP's masthead, range and starboard (the right side of the ship facing the bow) running lights were observed 15-20 degrees off KENNEDY's port bow.

MISTAKE NUMBER ONE:

The situation was clearly approaching "extremis" at that time ("extremis" means the point at which an action by either ship is unlikely to avoid collision).

However, carriers hold "flight ops" to be a very high priority (and rightly so, with aircraft needing a place to land). They expect cruisers and destroyers to "get out of the way" when they are coming to or on flight course. At this point, however, it was clear that BELKNAP was maneuvering erratically and unable to "get out of the way."

The international rules of the road, Article 7, state:

Vessels must use all available means to determine the risk of a collision, including the use of radar (if available) to get early warning of the risk of collision by radar plotting or equivalent systematic observation of detected objects.

If the distance of any vessel is reducing and her compass bearing is not changing much or it is a large vessel or towing vessel at close distance, or if there is any doubt, then a risk of collision shall be deemed to exist.

The rules further state that actions taken to avoid collision should be *positive, obvious and made in good time (read this as "early").*

It was now or never. Someone had to take action. Captain Gureck was on his bridge. Captain Shafer was not.

BELKNAP had not followed the carrier around remaining near her wake. Her display of a starboard running light meant that BELKNAP was ahead and just to the left of KENNEDY and her bow was pointed so as to cross in front of the carrier.

Captain Gureck noted that BELKNAP was 1200 yards away (actually it was more like 1500 yards) and saw her begin a turn to starboard. He saw both running lights, and then just the port running light.

BELKNAP appeared to come to a reciprocal course of that of the carrier.

This meant that if both ships held course, BELKNAP would pass close aboard KENNEDY's port side, but not necessarily collide. This passing distance between the two ships, in itself, was a cause for alarm.

Captain Gureck saw that BELKNAP had a left bearing drift and decreasing range. A left bearing drift means that the ship is moving to the left of the observing ship. A "steady" bearing drift, decreasing range would mean that she was coming "right at you." Decreasing range means just that; the ship is closing on you.

KENNEDY'S OOD estimated that BELKNAP would pass 1000-1200 yards on KENNEDY's port beam (far too close to be to a carrier). Normally, a cruiser or destroyer will remain outside the "123 box" around a carrier (1,000 yard astern, 2000 yards on each beam, 3,000 yards ahead) unless ordered closer for a maneuver such as replenishment at sea.

Captain Gureck ordered the conning officer to put the rudder amidships to check the swing of the ship and to steady on course 035 degrees (10 degrees short of the flight course of 025).

At 2156 (9:56 PM), BELKNAP was 1500 yards away from KENNEDY, on KENNEDY's port bow, showing BELKNAP's port bow to the carrier. Captain Gureck ordered the conning officer not to come further left until BELKNAP had passed CPA (closest point of approach).

At 2157, the officers on the bridge of KENNEDY saw BELKNAP's running lights again change; they saw both port and starboard running lights as BELKNAP apparently made a course change to the left (when you can see both port and starboard running lights of a ship, it means that she is headed directly at you). It was clear that BELKNAP was maneuvering erratically.

This course change by BELKNAP would take her directly in front of the oncoming carrier. KENNEDY did not change course or speed in response to seeing BELKNAP turn toward her bow.

MISTAKE NUMBER TWO.

In my opinion, the two ships were nearly in extremis at about 2158 (based on times reported in the hearing report). Collision was imminent. With a closing speed of about 17 knots (BELKNAP at about 5 knots, KENNEDY at about 12 knots), they had less than four minutes to stop in the 1200 remaining yards. That assumes they could stop. A large ship such as an aircraft carrier requires more than 1200 yards to stop, even backing full.

Captain Gureck directed KENNEDY's Communicator to transmit to BELKNAP over PRITAC "Interrogative your intentions."

BELKNAP responded, "Roger, my rudder is left, coming to course 190, speed 5 knots." (At speed 5 knots, a cruiser does not quickly respond to its rudder.)

Captain Gureck personally transmitted to BELKNAP

"Right full rudder." Here we have the Captain of one ship attempting to order the maneuver of another ship rather than control his own ship.

BELKNAP was now at a distance of about 1200 yards, with KENNEDY approximately 20 degrees on her starboard bow.

At about 2159 (9:59 PM), Captain Gureck took the conn and ordered "Right full rudder, all engines back full." The communicator transmitted to BELKNAP the rudder and engine order of KENNEDY. It would be too late.

When BELKNAP was about 600 yards away, she could be seen turning to starboard (Captain Shafer was now on the bridge of BELKNAP and had ordered the turn).

KENNEDY sounded the collision alarm (an alarm that alerts the crew that collision is imminent).

At 2200 (10:00 PM), BELKNAP began to pass down the port side of KENNEDY. Captain Gureck ordered left full rudder" so as to swing the carrier's stern away from BELKNAP.

The collision occurred at about 2201 (10:01 PM). BELKNAP's superstructure impacted the carrier's angled flight deck as the cruiser scraped down the port side of KENNEDY.

Aviation gas lines that ran under the flight deck were ruptured, pouring hundreds of gallons of volatile fluid down BELKNAP's stacks.

The damage to KENNEDY was serious in that it put her flight deck out of commission for several hours while the crew brought the fires under control. Superficially, the damage seemed not serious, but the fires destroyed a number of compartments and filled them with smoke.

It was fortunate that only one Sailor lost his life aboard KENNEDY that night. Had not Captain Shafer of BELKNAP turned in time, Kennedy's bow would have cut the cruiser in two with the certain loss of more life aboard both ships.

*****

Chapter Thirteen
On BELKNAP's Bridge

The report of the hearing noted that BELKNAP had no occasion in over a year to exercise in-close station keeping with a carrier until just prior to the collision, and that Lieutenant (Junior Grade) Kenneth M. Knull (BELKNAP's OOD at the time of the collision) had a reputation for being the "best OOD" in BELKNAP.

The hearing also noted that Junior Officer of the Deck (JOOD), Ensign Charles Howe, assumed the conn prior to the collision, and had no experience in close maneuvering situations.

At about 1845 (6:45 PM), BELKNAP received the signal to take station as a TACAN beacon and plane guard in the position previously noted. Captain Shafer was informed by the Officer of the Deck at the time, Lieutenant Walter R. Price.

At 1920 (7:20 PM), the carrier turned to port (left) to a course to the southwest (downwind), and BELKNAP successfully executed the turn, remaining approximately in station.

Lieutenant Junior Grade Knull assumed duties as OOD at about 1945. He placed a call to Captain Shafer informing him of the ship's station. Captain Shafer, who was in the wardroom watching a movie, acknowledged the assignment. Ensign Howe relieved as Junior Officer of the Deck and assumed the conn under the supervision of Lieutenant Junior Grade Knull.

At 2001 (8:01 PM), KENNEDY turned to starboard (right) to the northeast to launch aircraft (upwind). BELKNAP successfully executed the turn, following the carrier around, staying near her wake.

At 2115 (8:15 PM), KENNEDY executed a turn to starboard (right) to the south west (downwind). Again, BELKNAP successfully executed the turn.

At 2132 (9:32 PM), BELKNAP was on a course of 192 degrees at speed 10 knots.

MISTAKE NUMBER THREE.

When maneuvering within two miles of an aircraft carrier, the Captain needs to be on the bridge. He does not have to have the conn (control of the ship's helm and engines), but he should be where he is constantly aware of the tactical situation, prepared to assume the conn if "things get out of hand." Two miles leaves little room for error if there is a mistake by the OOD. This comes not from the benefit of hindsight, but from my own practice.

At 2149 (9:49 PM), BELKNAP acknowledged the signal from KENNEDY (who was the OTC, or Officer in Tactical Command of the main body formation consisting of KENNEDY and BELKNAP) to change course, coming to port (left) to course 025 degrees, speed 12.

At this time, the screening force under the tactical command of Commodore Schultz was in a circular sector screen around KENNEDY and BELKNAP. This force consisted of RICKETTS, DALE, PHARRIS, HART and BORDELON. Their designated stations were 5,000 to 8,000 yards from the formation guide (KENNEDY was formation guide, the ship that serves as a reference point for the formation) in sectors of fifty degrees each, RICKETTS and BORDELON to the north, PHARRIS, DALE and HART to the south.

These ships were conducting maneuvering and signal drills. When the main body changed course, all of these ships were on PRITAC and heard the course change, and were able to adjust their base course to correspond.

BELKNAP's JOOD had the conn, although he relied on the course and speed orders given to him by BELKNAP's OOD. The conning officer and the OOD sketched a rough maneuvering board (a plot used to calculate course and speed to change station) solution.

MISTAKE NUMBER FOUR.

BELKNAP was not changing station. It was a "corpen" signal that meant they were to maintain their relative position (station) astern of the carrier at 4000 yards. To do this, they had to "follow the carrier around in its turn."

Normal procedure for accomplishing this is to increase speed over base speed sufficiently to maneuver to the outside of the carrier's wake on the side away from the turn, and adjust course and speed to follow the carrier. This is more difficult to do at night, because the aspect of the carrier as she turns is not easily discernible. However, the first "move" is to turn away from the carrier in a direction opposite her turn.

Officers experienced in station keeping and maneuvering close to a carrier are well aware of this type of maneuver. Relying on a maneuvering board solution in this circumstance indicates (to me) that the officers in BELKNAP's bridge were inexperienced and had a poor understanding of relative motion.

The carrier's turn to flight course toward BELKNAP's station (left) instead of away from BELKNAP (right) as prior turns were accomplished, seems to have confused the young watch standers aboard BELKNAP.

The OOD's proposed maneuver was to slow to 5 knots and permit the carrier to pass in front of BELKNAP's bow, and then after the carrier proceeded down their port side, come left to station behind her.

The JOOD suggested coming to the new course immediately, and then slowing to allow KENNEDY to overtake BELKNAP, passing BELKNAP to starboard, and allowing BELKNAP to slide back into station.

Both the OOD's and the JOOD's proposed actions are, from the eyes of an experienced seaman, flawed. Both of them would result in BELKNAP being in front of the carrier, a place you don't want to be when you are at a distance of only a few miles (remember, on the scale of things at sea among large ships, a mile is a very short distance). Even if there had not been a collision, this maneuver would have created a "sticky situation" that would probably have resulted in BELKNAP being reprimanded.

BELKNAP's Command Information Center (CIC) was informed that the bridge intended to come "right" to course 025 at 5 knots and let the carrier overtake BELKNAP. The watch officer in CIC, Lieutenant Junior Grade John F. Hosner, concurred. All the officers on watch demonstrated a lack of understanding of what was happening and what should be done.

Meanwhile, Captain Shafer was still in the wardroom. He had not been informed of the course change or the proposed method of executing the change.

MISTAKE NUMBER FIVE.

This is quite unusual. All Captains' standing orders to his OOD's require them to notify him of any changes in formation, base course and speed.

The conning officer turned to port (left) contrary to the recommendation of CIC. The OOD took bearings on KENNEDY and noted very little bearing drift (which indicated that the ships were on collision courses). He ordered the conning officer to steady up on course 185, well short of the signaled new course of 025. This seems to further reflect his indecision.

CIC saw that a course of 185 would result in a close CPA to the carrier and recommended over the sound powered phone circuit to the bridge that the ship come right with full rudder to the new course (025 degrees). This recommendation was sent to the bridge on the JL circuit (a sound powered telephone circuit) to a Sailor manning those phones on the bridge. The recommendation was not passed to the OOD, the fault of the Sailor manning the circuit (lack of understanding or inexperience, or both).

The people in CIC are inside the ship without visual reference to what is occurring. They rely on data from the surface search radar, and on maneuvering board solutions. Any experienced OOD understands this and should take recommendations from CIC only with this understanding. This recommendation from CIC would, once again, place BELKNAP ahead of the carrier (on her bow). It did have one big advantage; by coming right (vice left) to the new course, it would turn away from the carrier, opening the range somewhat and possibly avoiding the collision.

The OOD decided to accept the recommendation and turn right. He ordered the conning officer to come right to course 025. At 2149 (9:40 PM), BELKNAP's conning officer (still the JOOD), ordered all engines ahead one third (5 knots), come right to course 025 degrees (the signaled course).

During the turn, the OOD observed KENNEDY moving from right to left and ordered the conning officer to "steady up" on course 220.

A cruiser at 5 knots turns very slowly with only five degrees rudder. If they were going to execute a change in course to 025 instead of following the carrier around, it should have been done with a speed at least equal to the carrier's speed, preferably more, and with at least an initial order of right standard rudder so as to open the range to the turning carrier. As it was, they were turning very slowly, and as the carrier turned toward them, the range was decreasing.

At this point, the OOD became visually confused. He thought he was looking at the starboard bow of the carrier (in actuality, he was seeing her port bow). The port and starboard running lights of KENNEDY were obscured by the many lights she had on preparing to land aircraft.

Lieutenant Junior Grade Knull queried Ensign Howe about what he was "seeing." Ensign Howe replied that he thought he saw her port bow, but wasn't sure.

A prudent OOD should recognize when he has "lost the picture" and summon the Captain to the bridge. He did not.

The OOD queried several personnel on the bridge as to what they thought the target angle of the carrier was (or, what view of the carrier were they "seeing"; her stern, her bow, her beam…?) No one could determine the target angle.

An aircraft carrier is a big, boxy looking structure at sea. Even in daylight, it takes an experienced seaman's eye to determine what "part" of the carrier is visible. Is she going away, coming toward, and so forth. At night, the situation is further confused by a blur of red (sometimes white) hangar and flight deck lights. Even in clear weather, what could be seen was a dark shape with no clear bow or stern and a blur of red lights.

The port lookout (usually a Seaman, or junior Sailor) reported KENNEDY's bearing three or four times as the ships approached each other. He also reported (5-10 minutes prior to the collision) that he saw a target angle of 350 degrees (this meant that he was seeing the carrier's port running light, and that BELKNAP was ten degrees on the carrier's port bow).

But...the OOD thought he was seeing the starboard bow of KENNEDY and ordered left standard rudder, speed twenty knots. He thought this action would clear BELKNAP to starboard of KENNEDY. Instead, it took BELKNAP directly toward KENNEDY.

MISTAKE NUMBER SIX.

BELKNAP's OOD went from one side of the bridge to the other, peering at the carrier, trying to determine her target angle. It appears that he did not hear the report of the port lookout, did not understand it, or chose to ignore it.

There followed a confusing set of course and speed changes. First, a turn left to 130 degrees, then right to 200 degrees.

Now the two officers on the bridge had totally "lost the bubble". BELKNAP was headed directly across the carrier's bow at minimum distance. If they collided, BELKNAP would be sliced in two by KENNEDY's heavy hull.

At 2156, (9:56 PM), BELKNAP's OOD ordered the BMOW to pass the word over the 1MC "Captain to the bridge".

Shortly thereafter, the JOOD conning officer ordered "left full rudder."

Again, lack of experience shows. Turning to port (left) at this point is a turn toward the oncoming behemoth. Ship handling school teaches that in an emergency, turn away and back full. If in doubt, turn to starboard and back full (because rules of the road require that the normal passage of two ships heading toward each other should be port side to port side, i.e. both turn to starboard, or right, to avoid the other).

Further confusion; the BMOW relieved the helmsman because he thought he had heard "RIGHT full rudder." He did so without permission of the conning officer (which is required).

MISTAKE NUMBER SEVEN.

The "presence" of an OOD on the bridge is very important. The bridge watch must have complete confidence in the officers on the bridge. If they see that the officers no longer have effective control of the ship, discipline breaks down and panic can follow.

Captain Shafer arrived on the bridge at 2157 (9:57 PM), a few seconds before Captain Gureck aboard KENNEDY transmitted the query "Interrogative your intentions."

The Captain stepped into a confused situation where no one knew what was occurring or what to do. On a dark bridge at night, it is difficult to adjust one's eyes immediately. It is also takes time, even for a man of the Captain's experience, to assess the situation and feel confident enough to take over."

The two ships were 1700-1800 yards apart at this time. BELKNAP was headed on a course that would cross KENNEDY's bow.

BELKNAP's CIC watch officer noted a left rudder deflection at about 1300 yards. He got on the 21MC (the "squawk box") to the bridge and recommended right full rudder. The bridge did not acknowledge this recommendation.

The OOD told Captain Shafer that KENNEDY had crossed BELKNAP's bow and that he didn't know what her target angle (aspect) was.

The Captain looked out and could see KENNEDY a short distance away on BELKNAP's starboard bow.

He queried the OOD as to what course KENNEDY was coming to (025 degrees).

At 2158 (9:58 PM), Captain Shafer did not take note of Captain Gureck's transmission over PRITAC for BELKNAP to apply "right full rudder". Nor was he required to. Though it was "what should be done," Captain Gureck had the responsibility to maneuver his own ship, not BELKNAP.

BELKNAP did not sound any general quarters or collision alarms.

MISTAKE NUMBER EIGHT.

At 2159 (9:59 PM), BELKNAP's OOD ordered "left full rudder, all engines ahead flank (25 knots)" and by so doing assumed the conn. Captain Shafer had been on the bridge for two minutes and still had not assumed the conn, still unsure of the situation.

A basic rule of ship handling is "when in doubt, all engines stop, rudder amidships". In other words, "start all over."

The order given would have increased the speed with which BELKNAP crossed the bow of KENNEDY, which might have given her a better chance of clearing, but just barely. It was a risky order, because it takes a minute or so for a steam turbine ship to attain the screw revolutions for 25 knots (and in fact they were not attained). It is not clear whether or not this order would have avoided collision. In any case, crossing a carrier's bow at very short range is a potentially disastrous maneuver.

At about the same time, Captain Shafer concluded he was "seeing" a port aspect of the carrier and that the ships were in extremis.

Captain Shafer made a snap decision. He saw that the current course and speed would result in BELKNAP being struck by KENNEDY amidships. He ordered "right full rudder, all engines back emergency full."

The ship leaned to starboard and shuddered as the big screws churned the water.

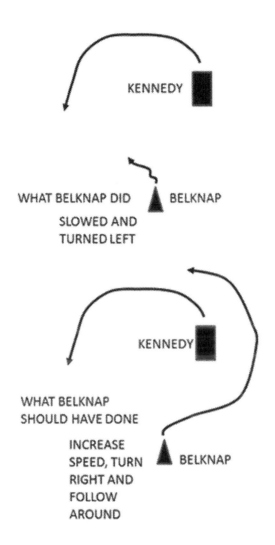

BELKNAP's bow swung precariously to starboard, toward the bow of KENNEDY. Breaths were held as the bow passed KENNEDY's bow and swung along her port side. There was a chance, a slim one, that the Captain's actions would save the ship.

The bow scraped along KENNEDY's side. Then, the cruiser heeled hard to port. From the bridge, they looked up and saw the big angled flight deck structure rushing toward them.

There was a crashing, buckling sound as everyone ducked and braced themselves.

KENNEDY's flight deck tore through BELKNAP's superstructure just above the bridge. Then, a loud explosion sent a shock wave through the ship as aviation fuel from ruptured lines poured down BELKNAP's stacks and exploded in the fiery heat.

*****

Chapter Fourteen
KENNEDY After the Collision

The initial contact aboard KENNEDY occurred port side at the forward edge of the flight deck extension. The ships were in physical contact for up to three minutes.

General quarters (Condition I) was set immediately. Sailors ran through smoky compartments to set Material Condition "Z" (watertight with fire barriers between compartments). It was set in the vicinity of the fires within 10 minutes.

Fires broke out aboard KENNEDY in compartments from the main deck to the 03 level and in the compartments under the angled deck. Large amounts of heavy smoke from BELKNAP's fires were sucked into the carrier's main living spaces and engineering spaces. Fires were lost in two boilers and one engine (one of four screws) was off line.

All of KENNEDY's fixed wing aircraft scheduled to land at 2200 were diverted to the Naval Air Facility at Sigonella, Sicily. Helicopters were able to operate from the flight deck soon as soon as the major fires were out. HS-11's Sea Kings flew over 36 hours of support flights during the search and rescue operations, transferring 88 men, including 17 litter patients and 60 injured Sailors.

PHARRIS was assigned by Commodore Schultz to assist KENNEDY's fire fighting efforts. However, she was unable to get close enough to the fires to be effective due to the overhang of the carrier's flight deck.

KENNEDY came to "all stop" to allow engineering spaces to be ventilated and re-manned. Captain Gureck then ordered "all engines ahead two thirds" to clear BELKNAP. Only number one shaft (propeller) responded due to smoke ingestion by personnel in the other engine rooms.

As BELKNAP crunched down KENNEDY's port side, her superstructure cut into three external aviation fuel risers. Two of these were charged with fuel (under pressure). Fuel poured from these severed lines at the rate of about 1045 gallons per minute onto BELKNAP. In the first several minutes, KENNEDY's Fuel Officer gave an order that took the pressure off the fuel lines.

On KENNEDY's flight deck, Sailors put water on BELKNAP as she slid down the side. The flight deck fire truck moved aft with BELKNAP, applying water as it went along.

KENNEDY lost fires in two of her boilers due to heavy smoke in the boiler room. This resulted in the loss of four turbo generators. The ventilation intakes on KENNEDY's port side sucked in smoke from the burning cruiser which resulted in the evacuation of the engineering spaces. Smoke filled the office and living spaces on the port side near the point of collision.

KENNEDY came to "all stop" about 6000 yards from BELKNAP. KENNEDY'S XO coordinated the fire fighting efforts. Fires on the flight deck and port side catwalks (walkways beside and just under the flight deck) were put out in the first ten minutes following the collision. Casualty control stations were manned and prepared for receiving mass casualties.

The main engineering spaces were re-manned at 2251 (10:51 PM). Despite the loss of several machinery spaces due to smoke ingestion, KENNEDY had enough machinery remaining on line such that power was never lost and fire fighting pressure remained available.

All fires on KENNEDY were reported out by 0031 (thirty-one minutes after midnight). Numerous re-flashes occurred and were quickly extinguished.

"Secure from General Quarters" wasn't sounded until 1100 (11:00 AM) the next day.

One man was killed aboard KENNEDY, a Yeoman who had been in a personnel office near the point of impact with BELKNAP.

There were many heroes on the carrier that night. Citations were awarded to Aviation Structural Mechanic (Structures) Third Class Raymond A. Pabon, Aviation Structural Mechanic (Structures) Airman William L. Snyder, and Aviation Structural Mechanic (Hydraulics) Third Class Harold T. Collier from VF-32.

Damage to the Leading Edge of KENNEDY'S Angled
Flight Deck
(World Wide Web Source)

Airman James D. Lunn, of VA-72, having been issued an oxygen breathing apparatus, grabbed a hose and climbed three levels to the source of a fire. Perceiving a dull red-orange glow of burning tires within thick black smoke, Lunn trained his hose upon it until an explosion blew him backwards through a hatch, depositing him three decks below in a foot of water. He was taken to sick bay and treated for burned hands and a lacerated right ear.

The damage to KENNEDY was serious in that it put her flight deck out of commission for several hours while the crew brought the fires under control. Superficially. the damage seemed not serious, but the fires destroyed a number of compartments and filled them with smoke.

It was fortunate that only one Sailor lost his life aboard KENNEDY that night. Had not Captain Shafer of

BELKNAP turned in time, Kennedy's bow would have cut the cruiser in two with the certain loss of more life aboard both ships.

Damage to the Port Side Midships Section of
KENNEDY'S Angled Flight Deck
(World Wide Web Source)

*****

KENNEDY'S officers and crew responded well to the emergency. The ship was back to operational status by the next morning.

*****

Chapter Fifteen
BELKNAP After the Collision:

Contact was made with KENNEDY in the vicinity of BELKNAP's frame 78. A "frame" is a rib that is part of the skeleton of a ship. The frames act as stiffeners, holding the outside plating in shape and maintaining the transverse form of the ship.

The port side of BELKNAP's bridge at the 03 level and the missile fire control director platform above the bridge took the brunt of the initial contact. The port side of the ship in the vicinity of sonar and computer control was crushed inward.

The collision ruptured aviation fuel risers (pipes that carry fuel from below decks to topside aircraft refueling stations) on KENNEDY'S port side. Aviation fuel rained down on BELKNAP. There were explosions and dense black smoke. The ship listed heavily to port amid the grinding, screeching sounds of metal on metal.

BELKNAP's boiler fires were extinguished by fire and explosion shortly after the backing bell was answered. There were severe explosions in the after two engineering spaces. They were the direct cause of most of the injuries and deaths aboard BELKNAP. There was a momentary loss of electrical power and fire main pressure before the emergency diesel generators started.

All the engineering spaces were evacuated. BELKNAP had no power except for her emergency diesel generators. Heavy smoke throughout the ship made movement difficult, if not impossible. Sailors groped their way to their emergency stations. Enough of them found their way to hatches and valves to set Material Condition "Z". Setting this condition resulted in sealing off the magazines in the forward and after parts of the ship. This quick reaction helped to save the ship from explosions that would probably have resulted in her sinking.

Three groups of BELKNAP men organized themselves into fire fighting parties; one on the bridge, one on the foc'sle and one on the fantail. The middle part of the ship was impassable as flames roared high in the night air. Sailors aft were totally cut off from their Shipmates in the forward part of the ship.

The emergency generators began to fail, as did several of the fire pumps that provided fire fighting water.

*****

Captain Shafer remained on the bridge and directed fire fighting efforts as best he could without effective communications within the ship. He and his watch standers took cover as the 3"/50 gun ammunition, CHAFFROC and pyrotechnics "cooked off" amidships.

At about 2205 (10:05 PM), RICKETTS could be seen approaching BELKNAP's starboard side, bow to BELKNAP's stern. At about 2215 (10:15 PM), RICKETTS was close enough to send a shower of water onto the fires raging in the amidships area of BELKNAP.

Captain Shafer and his crew fought the fires valiantly through the night, assisted by the crew of RICKETTS and the other ships of Destroyer Squadron TWENTY-TWO.

BELKNAP the Next Morning, After the Collision
(Photograph by Dennis Eaves)

Top Down View, Damage to BELKNAP's Bridge Area
(World Wide Web Source)

Damage to BELKNAP's Starboard Side
(Photograph by Dennis Eaves)

Stern View of BELKNAP
(Photograph by Dennis Eaves)

Port Side Aft of BELKNAP After the Collision and Fire
(Photograph by Dennis Eaves)

Seven men were killed aboard BELKNAP, four in the vicinity of the after engine room and three near sonar and computer control on the port side aft of the bridge area (which was crushed by the impact with KENNEDY). Forty-seven others were injured and evacuated for treatment.

*****

The following morning, we had our first good look at what remained of BELKNAP. It is hard to express my feelings at the time. Depression. Pride. Exhaustion. Thankfulness. Admiration. A flood of emotions that still come back to me as I write. A Sailor grows to love his ship, no matter how hard the job or how demanding the voyage. To see a proud warship dismasted and charred struck at my inner self. It couldn't help but shake one's confidence in facing future voyages.

I shook it off. I was the Captain; the officers and crew depended on me, and there was more to be done

*****

Chapter Sixteen
The Long Voyage Home

As the investigation continued, BELKNAP Sailors threw a party for RICKETTS Sailors at the Merchant Seaman's Club in Naples. It was quite an emotional affair. The CVR Band had played there before, and played again that night. They were, as usual, really good. They lit up the place with rock n' roll and country. Ray Jones and Ron Morin were the featured singers. Dennis Eaves was the Master of ceremonies. There were even a few women to dance with, but as the wine and beer flowed freely, everyone was dancing, solo or otherwise.

BELKNAP's Sailors honored RICKETTS Sailors and thanked us. They presented me with a BELKNAP jacket and ball cap.

It was a very emotional time for me. The outflow of gratitude was sincere and the sense of camaraderie strong.

A thought from Phil Coady; "I recall many of us commenting at the time that you would remember that recognition from the crew of BELKNAP longer than any award the Navy might give you for the rescue."

He was right.

*****

Phil came to me on the morning after the party. He was all grins. "Captain, be careful what you ask the crew to do, 'cause right now they'd do anything you say."

I smiled. It was a sobering thought after all we'd been through. "It looks like all I have to do is ask them to be themselves."

We chatted awhile. I told Phil how much I appreciated what he had done. I knew all the officers and chiefs had pitched in and "been there" when something was needed. But it was Phil's energy and knowledge that "ran the ship" while I was engaged in maneuvering.

"You know, Phil, the thing I'm proudest of, amidst all

the things that happened, was that I was able to devote one hundred per cent of my attention to the conn with full confidence that things within the ship that must be done would be."

"I had a lot of help."

"The time you, Dave Ricketts and I spent training the officers and crew and building a disciplined and proud crew really paid off."

"Remember when you told me that the real work is done in port and in training, getting ready, and that if you're ready, things at sea will work out?"

"I do."

"We have the proof."

*****

The investigation found that the damage to RICKETTS was not "mission limiting". It was confined to internal hull frames, decks and bulkheads on the port side between frames 65 and 115, and external damage to the superstructure port and starboard weather break and bulwark.

Most of the damage was sustained during the third approach when we were actually moored to BELKNAP. It was a remarkable testament to the construction of a DDG-2 class ship and the HY-80 steel hull. After the event, Steve and his engineers cut the crushed sections out and the hull and the steam lines essentially went back to their original alignment. The integrity testing we did showed that all was okay. We would continue the deployment.

The officers had an aluminum section of the crushed port break cut away and made into a lamp, which was later presented to me.

*****

We were on the final few months of our deployment. On December 9, we anchored off the harbor of Barcelona, Spain.

Barcelona was always one of my favorite ports in the Med. Spanish culture, great restaurants, beautiful promenades. I could sit for hours in the evening at a sidewalk café drinking Tio Pepe (a very dry Spanish Sherry), eating bread and calameras fritas (fried squid).

The officers and crew had some great times ashore. I tried, but I couldn't shake the memories of the collision. I had been lucky that night. I felt like I was living on the edge.

*****

On 15 December, we left Barcelona to participate in an anti-air warfare exercise with the Spanish Navy.

Being underway again was a relief and I immersed myself in the action. Spirits aboard were high. The officers and crew were proud of their accomplishments and the time to head back to our loved ones was fast approaching.

*****

On 22 December, we moored at Palma de Mallorca, Spain. Mallorca is a beautiful Spanish Island in the western Mediterranean Sea. We were scheduled to spend Christmas there.

Christmas overseas without your family seems like an empty holiday. Once again, a Spanish port offered a pleasant, relaxing time, and the crew enjoyed a good liberty.

Just before Christmas, Captain Richard (Dick) K. Albright reported aboard as the Commodore's relief. On 27 January, RICKETTS hosted the change of command ceremony for Commander, Destroyer Squadron TWENTY-TWO.

We rented a place in the city and threw a party for Milt. He was presented with a silver punch bowl and a cup with the name of each of his ships engraved on it.

Milt was on his way home, and we had a new Commodore. Dick was a capable guy, and we got along well.

*****

On 7 January, we visited Malaga, Spain. Malaga is a beautiful and interesting port situated on Spain's southern *Costa Del Sol (Coast of the Sun)*. We entered a narrow passage through a breakwater and moored at a pier in the heart of downtown. It was hot and the wine was terrific.

By this time, I was, for the most part, over my post Belknap blues. I enjoyed Malaga.

Then, our schedule changed. We were ordered to conduct a port visit to Lisbon, Portugal prior to sailing for Norfolk. There was a diplomatic need to visit Portugal to demonstrate continuing U.S. friendship. It was a last minute "show the flag" mission.

*****

On 14 January, we were off Lisbon. The port was socked in with an impenetrable fog. Our designated mooring was at a pier on the other side of a bridge. It looked simple on the chart. It wasn't.

I decided to proceed into port using radar navigation. I posted fog lookouts on the foc'sle and made sure I had my best people on watch. Garry was the OOD. Phil was on the bridge backing everyone up.

We proceeded slowly into a wide mouthed estuary that turned into the Rio Tejo which led to Lisbon. On radar, I could see the channel buoys. I could also see large blips that indicated anchored ships on either side of the channel. We "felt" our way down the channel relying on radar navigation and instinct.

On either side of us sounded the bells of ships at anchor (required to ring when anchored in fog). The visibility was such that I could see the bow of my ship, but not much more. On one occasion, I heard a bell that seemed to be above my line of sight from the bridge. Something BIG was anchored there, but I couldn't see it.

As we approached the bridge across the river, which we couldn't see, there came a report from a lookout that still draws a smile when I correspond with my officers.

"Sir, train crossing, dead ahead, moving from starboard to port.

"Very well."

We heard the train but never saw it. We passed under the bridge without seeing it or the train.

Garry had the conn. I was right behind him. Finally we saw the assigned pier. It was actually a long wharf that ran parallel to the shore. There were no tugs to be seen.

Garry made an approach on the pier. The current was running so strong that we had great difficulty getting a heaving line over. As soon as our bow approached the wharf and a heaving line was thrown, the current would grab the hull and push us away. I estimated the current to be 5-6 knots.

We pulled away from the wharf, twisted around and made another approach. Now the current grabbed us and shoved us at the pier. Garry had to back two thirds to keep from slamming into the pier.

"Captain," said Phil from behind me, "we kicked up a little mud that time, maybe you should take it."

At that point I needed no further encouragement. It was clear that I had to take the conn. I did.

I twisted around and lined up for another approach, this time into the current again. I hollered down at Chief Pugh on the foc'sle.

"I'm going to get the bow close to the pier and hold it there. I want that first heaving line to count!"

Chief Pugh went to the Sailor with the heaving line, took it from him and looked up at me expectantly.

I used an ahead two thirds bell to approach the wharf (normally, a one third bell is used when maneuvering around a pier). The bow was only ten to twenty yards away from the wharf when I ordered "all engines ahead one third." The bow drifted toward the pier, then the current grabbed the ship and the ahead one third bell held her in place.

Chief Pugh made a mighty heave. The line sailed toward the pier.

"Get number one line over, hold it, and put it on the capstan (a large, electric powered winch used for hauling in the anchor as well as mooring lines)."

We got the number one line over and hauled in on the capstan, drawing the bow to the wharf. Once I had the bow under control (with number one line), I twisted the ship into the wharf with opposed engines, got the rest of the lines over and held the ship to the pier.

"Double up all lines and put out a wire fore and aft."

After we were moored, I was whisked off in a car to visit with the local dignitaries. We shared a glass of port. It tasted good after that landing.

That night, the officers invited me out to visit a supposedly good watering hole with them. But, that trip through the fog and the tough landing left me exhausted and had me "thinking" again. I passed.

*****

We were ready to leave Lisbon and head back to Norfolk. The Special Sea Detail was set. I was on the bridge.

A Portuguese pilot reported aboard and a tug chugged off my starboard bow, ready to "make fast."

I wasn't sure I needed or wanted a pilot. Particularly one who didn't speak English. My Spanish language training allowed me to welcome him in words he understood.

The tug was made fast to my starboard bow. I invited the pilot to take the conn.

We took in all lines and the pilot began to issue orders. He backed the engines. Immediately, we began to gather stern way. Then that strong current grabbed the ship: a lot of movement astern.

We were on the port wing of the bridge. I looked back. Moored behind us was a merchant ship. We were underway and backing toward her!

"This is the Captain. I have the conn. All engines stop."

I indicated to the pilot that he should take his tug

and leave. He was very displeased. I don't know if I destroyed the diplomatic purpose of the port visit, but, in the meantime, my ship was about to collide with the merchant ship astern.

"All engines ahead two thirds."

White water boiled at my stern. I could see that it wasn't going to be enough.

"All engines ahead standard."

In the engine room, they responded quickly. Later Steve told me, "when I hear 'take in all lines,' followed almost immediately by an ahead standard bell, I know something is wrong. We held our breath."

I held the standard bell until I saw that we had enough headway to avoid the ship astern.

"All engines ahead one third."

The pilot was in the pilot house talking frantically to Bill Doud. Bill later told me, "he was afraid you were going to swamp his tug."

I motioned to Bill to get the pilot off the ship, and in a hurry. I held the ship into the current with a one third bell until the pilot and his tug were away and clear.

Fortunately, there was no fog. I turned the ship and we passed under the bridge and out to sea without further incident.

I had avoided a bullet. I'd had it with pilots!

*****

On 27 January, after an uneventful Atlantic crossing, we approached the harbor of Hampton Roads (Norfolk). A thick fog greeted us. Another one.

Somewhere, someone was plotting to present me with challenges at every port, it seemed.

I had a choice. I could anchor outside the channel until the fog lifted. Or, I could proceed into port using radar navigation. I knew that the families waited for us at the pier. I fantasized that there would be some sort of special welcome upon our return; some acknowledgement of what the ship had accomplished. No glory to the faint of heart. I decided to proceed into the pier.

This time, it was a bit different. I knew the channel into Norfolk like the palm of my hand. I had navigated it in RICKETTS and in other ships and boats many times.

We went between the two bridge-tunnel islands, over the tunnel and into Thimble Shoals channel. It was a straight channel all the way to Fort Wool where there was a tricky turn to port into the Norfolk Harbor Reach.

This was where the battleship USS MISSOURI (BB-63) had run aground on 17 January, 1950. It had taken until 1 February to get her off the sand bar. My father had been one of the Navy lawyers that handled the subsequent investigation. I did not want to repeat the battleship's event.

As we approached Fort Wool, it was an eerie sight. The fog lay like a low blanket across Hampton Roads. I could just barely see my bow. But I could clearly see the top floors of the Hotel Chamberlain at Fort Story. The hotel stuck out of the fog like the residence of some angel resting on a cloud.

I made the turn at Foot Wool and saw on the radar a large "blip" in Norfolk Harbor Reach. This "skunk" was headed out while I was headed in. I edged over to the far right of the channel and passed inboard of a buoy. I watched the "skunk" on radar. She had a good left bearing drift. The CPA would be a few hundred yards to port. I walked to the port bridge wing and strained my eyes to see the oncoming ship; passed my intentions to her over channel 16 (international maneuvering circuit). The skunk and my ship passed port to port without ever seeing each other.

I approached the pier based on a radar contact of the area. My berth was starboard side to the pier. The current was running a few knots on an incoming tide, which meant it would sweep me past the pier if I miscalculated my turn.

No tugs were seen or offered. I guess it was too foggy for them. Anyway, in those days, it was considered demeaning for a destroyer Captain to admit to needing a tug.

RICKETTS as Seen From the Pier Arriving Home in Norfolk, Virginia Through a Thick Fog (RICKETTS Cruise Book Photograph)

At the last minute, I saw the pier and the families huddled there waiting for us. I was told later that a cheer went up as they saw the lean, gray destroyer break out of the fog, old glory at her mast, blue and gold "pretty birds" (dummy missiles used for testing) run up on the arms of her missile launcher. I didn't hear it, as I saw what I feared. If I didn't act, we would be swept by the pier by the current.

"All engines ahead two thirds."

I was headed for the pier with ten knots rung up. The angle looked about right. I just had to get inside the piers and away from that current.

"All engines back full."

The engines threw up a white wake at my stern as the ship glided toward the pier. I watched the water flow beside the ship. You have to stop those engines at just the right time, or you'll get stern way and find yourself out in the channel again.

"All engines stop."

RICKETTS glided beside the pier and stopped. Heaving lines went over. Then the meesnger lines followed by the main lines which were made fast. I had to give her a little nudge with an ahead one third bell to achieve proper position on the pier.

After all the kudos we had received, I expected at least one of the Admirals in command in Norfolk at the time to greet us at homecoming and congratulate the ship. At least, a representative from higher command. I was disappointed. It didn't happen.

I saw Phyllis on the pier with our son Bruce and daughter Carolyn. I waved. They waved back.

We were home.

Families and Friends Greet RICKETTS and Her Crew at the Pier in Norfolk, Virginia Upon Return from the Mediterranean Sea

*****

There were many heroes the night of the collision. A list of the awards presented is included at the end of the book. Phil, the Department Heads and Division Officers had their hands full deciding who was to receive an award and why. It was a difficult task, given the many who contributed so bravely that night.

Of special note are the four men who received the Navy and Marine Corps Medal for Lifesaving: Lieutenant Junior Grade Greg Geist, whose knowledge and courage was primarily responsible for the many damage control efforts that went on that night; Chief Boatswain's Mate Jerry Pugh, the hero of the exposed and dangerous foc'sle, whose leadership and presence resulted in pouring immense amounts of water on the fires amid exploding ammunition; Chief Hospital Corpsman Jim Coleman, whose brave climb to the foc'sle of BELKNAP in heavy seas and the emergency medical attention he gave badly burned and injured Sailors saved many lives; and Petty Officer First Class (Hull Technician) Randolph McClary, who, while at the forefront of the all the damage control efforts in exposed and dangerous conditions throughout the ship, assisted BELKNAP's men in extinguishing fires.

McClary's story took a special twist once we got back to Norfolk. When I had assumed command, McClary was a Petty Officer Second Class. At the time of the BELKNAP collision, he was a Petty Officer First Class.

It was time to nominate Sailors for the Commander-in Chief U.S. Atlantic Fleet (CINCLANTFLT) Sailor of the Year award. The choice was clear. I nominated Petty Officer McClary.

Phil and I, with the assistance of the Chief Petty Officers, Steve and Greg, tutored McClary for the interviews he would have to undergo, staged mock interviews, and in general advised him what he should do to help win the award.

McClary took to the tutoring in the same professional way he handled his job; with a smile and hard work. He practiced the interviews. He bought new uniforms and prepared himself for the big day. His shipmates rooted for him. And then...

McClary won!

With it came automatic promotion to Chief Petty Officer. In the brief span of a year and a half, he had gone from Petty Officer Second Class to Chief Petty Officer. Quite a success story.

He was a special Sailor.

Petty Officer First Class Randolph McClary and Captain Powers Discuss the Nomination as CINCLANTFLT Sailor of the Year.

*****

Chapter Seventeen
Analysis of the Collision

On 27 January, a court martial was begun for Captain Shafer and Lieutenant Junior Grade Knull (BELKNAP's OOD). Captain Gureck and Lieutenant Commander Vester (KENNEDY's OOD) were never brought to court martial.

It was ironic that the court martial was held at the Norfolk Naval Legal Center in the "Rear Admiral Robert Davis Powers, Jr. Court Room" (dedicated just before the court martial in honor of my father).

Captain Shafer was found not guilty of criminal charges. Lieutenant Junior Grade Knull was found guilty and held accountable.

Navy Times, May 9, 1988, in an article titled "At Sea, a Vestige of Absolute Accountability", reported the following:

After the BELKNAP tragedy, a naval court of inquiry found the commanding officer responsible, but he was acquitted of criminal negligence charges by court martial. Perceiving this could cause confusion over the issue of command accountability, Admiral James F. Holloway III, then Chief of Naval Operations, sent a memorandum "to all flag officers and officers in command" stressing the Navy was not softening on the issue. Holloway said while BELKNAP's captain was not found criminally responsible, he was not absolved of his responsibility as a commanding officer.

The commander's responsibility for his command is absolute and he must and will be held accountable for its safety, well being and efficiency," Holloway said. "In some cases, commanders will be called upon to answer for their conduct in a court of law. In all cases, they will be professionally judged by seagoing officers – a far more stringent accountability in the eyes of those who follow the sea."

I am sure that Captain Shafer felt himself "fully accountable."

*****

Overall, KENNEDY ordered a formation that most likely contributed to the collision. Additionally, at least eight major mistakes were made that contributed to the collision. Three can be attributed to KENNEDY; six to BELKNAP. These mistakes are summarized in the following paragaphs.

*****

KENNEDY"S MISTAKES

The Formation: Plane Guard Assignment:

KENNEDY "took" BELKNAP from the screen and assigned her to replace PHARRIS as plane guard. This was probably unnecessary. The visibility was 10 miles. The cloud cover was scattered and broken and ranged from 2,000 to 7,00 feet. A returning aircraft homing on BELKNAP's TACAN could distinguish between the cruiser and the carrier, Given the known inexperience of BELKNAP at plane guarding, the formation would have been better served and all operational needs satisfied if PHARRIS had been left as plane guard and BELKNAP assigned as TACAN beacon while in the screen 3-4 miles from the carrier. This arrangement could have been easily communicated to returning aircraft.

Though carriers are used to choosing their own course and speed and expect cruisers and destroyers to "avoid them", it is clear under the international rules of the road that when ships are approaching extremis, they BOTH have the responsibility to maneuver to avoid collision.

First Opportunity to Avoid Collision:

The following observations are based on information in the Hearing Report.

At approximately 2156 (9:56 PM) BELKNAP's masthead, range and starboard running lights were observed 15-20 degrees off KENNEDY's port bow. The situation was approaching "extremis" at that time.

Captain Gureck saw BELKNAP begin a turn to starboard. He saw both running lights, and then just the port running light. He noted a left bearing drift with decreasing range. Rather than assuming the conn and turning away, he ordered the conning officer to put the rudder amidships to check the swing of the ship and not to come further left until BELKNAP had passed CPA (closest point of approach).

At 2157, he saw BELKNAP's running lights again change; he saw both port and starboard running lights as BELKNAP apparently made a course change to the left. This was a clear indication that BELKNAP would pass directly in front of the oncoming carrier unless action was taken. No action was taken by KENNEDY.

Second Opportunity to Avoid Collision:

At about 2158 (based on times reported in the hearing report) Captain Gureck directed KENNEDY's Communicator to transmit to BELKNAP over PRITAC "Interrogative your intentions."

BELKNAP responded, "Roger, my rudder is left, coming to course 190, speed 5 knots."

At about 2159, Captain Gureck personally transmitted to BELKNAP "Right full rudder." No speed or rudder orders were issued to the helm aboard KENNEDY at this time. BELKNAP was now at a distance of about 1200 yards, with KENNEDY about 20 degrees on her starboard bow.

Shortly thereafter, Captain Gureck took the conn and ordered "Right full rudder, all engines back full."

It was too late.

*****

BELKNAP's MISTAKES

There were at least six major mistakes made by BELKNAP:

Captain on the Bridge

Captain Shafer was not on BELKNAP's bridge until too late. The Captain of a ship should, in my opinion, always be on the bridge for major evolutions, particularly when maneuvering in close proximity to other ships.

The OOD's Flawed Solution

BELKNAP's OOD chose a flawed solution to execute a "corpen" signal, a turn in which ships are to maintain their same relative position to one another. He turned toward the carrier's turn and slowed when he should have turned away and increased speed to "follow the carrier around."

Failure to Keep the Captain Informed

BELKNAP's OOD did not inform Captain Shafer of the signaled turn, its execution or his intended action. There are many things happening on the bridge in maneuvering situations. Lieutenant Junior Grade Knull was supervising Ensign Howe (who had the conn). He was busy. Still, he should have called the Captain to inform him what was going on. Had he done that, it is likely that Captain Shafer would have been on the bridge much earlier.

The Lookout's Report

BELKNAP's OOD ignored, or did not hear, a lookout's accurate report of the carrier's aspect. Lookouts are trained to see the target angle (aspect) of other ships. In the confusion on BELKNAP's bridge, a lookout correctly reported the port bow aspect of the carrier, but the report was not acknowledged or utilized.

Command Presence

BELKNAP's OOD lost his command presence on the bridge. When the Captain is not on the bridge, the OOD is his direct representative, and is responsible to the Captain for handling the ship. When the OOD "loses it", the confidence level on the bridge goes rapidly down and confusion can result.

Orders to the Helm

BELKNAP's OOD issued orders to the helm while in a state of confusion and panic. As soon as he "lost the bubble" (when he lost visual understanding of the situation), he should have called the Captain to the bridge. Orders issued when "not sure" are erroneous orders.

*****

MY MISTAKE

My mistake that night was in remaining too long alongside BELKNAP after the third approach when we moored to her. I should have insisted that we stand clear once all the injured men were cleared from BELKNAP's foc'sle.

Had I done so, the damage to the ship might have been less. I was very fortunate that the damage was not more severe and that no one in my crew was seriously injured.

I could have backed off, stood by, and gone alongside again if BELKNAP had needed more assistance. The problem was, BELKNAP was without fire fighitng water pressure and fires were re-flashing.

Why did I stay longer? To provide the wter pressure. And, after several hours alongside, I got used to it, and it seemed less dangerous than it actually was. I now recognize that as every minute passed, the situation was becoming more dangerous to my ship and my crew.

In hindsight, we all could have done better.

Things happen.

*****

In the investigation, Captain Shafer stated that he would not have gone to the bridge had he been notified and had he concurred in the OOD's plan. He considered the OOD at the time to be his most reliable OOD.

Of course, the Captain wasn't notified in a timely way, and had he been briefed on the OOD's "plan", he no doubt would have been on the bridge quickly, for it was, to an experienced seaman, a flawed plan. A Captain must be able to recognize quickly when he must "step in." When that decision is made, he must act decisively. Captain Shafer did not have that opportunity because he chose to not be on the bridge, and because his "best OOD" did not keep him informed.

A station on a maneuvering carrier at 4000 yards is closer than a cruiser should be normally be, although I have been in similar stations many times on a destroyer. If the maneuver required when the carrier turns is to turn with her, maintaining TRUE bearing, it is not difficult. One simply turns to the new course. Even then, you'd better keep a wary eye on the larger ship, as carriers "seeking the wind" have been known to signal one course and end up on another. Their turning characteristics are much different than a cruiser or destroyer (slower, wider).

If the maneuver required when the carrier turns is to maintain RELATIVE bearing on the carrier (such as turn and remain astern of the carrier and to the left of her wake as was the case with BELKNAP), it's a completely different story.

I have been in "plane guard" station as close as 1200 yards behind the carrier and to port of her wake. It is actually easier to follow her around when you are closer, as you can see her better and see her wake clearly.

The range between ships can close quickly from a station only 1200 yards astern. When you are that close, you have to "watch it", because, as noted, carriers don't always signal their course and speed changes as they seek the wind (of course, they should, but any destroyerman at the time and he will tell you they frequently didn't, maybe still don't). Carrier crews assume that cruisers and destroyers will look out for themselves. And we did. Mostly.

Knowing all this and being informed of the station BELKNAP was to take, I would have chosen to be on the bridge, even with my most experienced OOD. BELKNAP's OOD may have been a very good watch officer in routine maneuvering situations. This was not, in my opinion, routine. And, through the OOD's actions, he demonstrated that he had a poor understanding of the relative motion between ships in a close-in maneuvering situation.

Captain Shafer also stated that he did not believe that a maneuvering board solution was required to execute the course change. In fact, a successful maneuvering board solution was never completed. On this subject, we agree.

In fact, attempting to execute the course change based on a maneuvering board solution may have contributed to the collision. There is no maneuvering board solution for "following the carrier around" in its turn. It requires a fine seaman's eye and a thorough understanding of the handling characteristics of both ships.

Maneuvering board solutions tend to be a "straight shots" of how to get from one relative position to another in fleet formations. They are not intended to solve problems of close-in maneuver involving ships with large turning radii (carriers) and smaller ships with completely different handling characteristics.

Captain Shafer also noted in the investigation that he always instructed his OODs to turn away from the carrier. His OOD failed to follow his orders.

The best instruction in ship handling is experience under the watchful eye of an experienced Captain. I went through that school. Many days and nights I would sit in the Captain's chair on the bridge and watch what the OODs did. I would occasionally coach, giving them a little hand signal; come left, come right, more speed, etc. At times, I dozed, but when I was needed, I was there.

I remember one OOD who asked, "Captain, how do you always know when to wake up?"

My answer, "I never really sleep; I'm just resting and listening."

Somehow, you learn to rest while your mind is attuned to what's going on around you. You hear the radio and the signals sent. You hear the orders to the helm and the engines. You hear the forced draft blowers increase or decrease speed. You "feel" the ship as it leans to port or starboard, accelerates or decelerates. If something doesn't "sound" or "feel" right, you are instantly fully awake. And it takes only a few moments to understand what's "wrong". But, you have to be on the bridge.

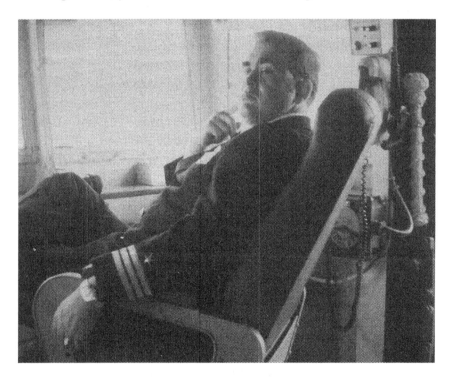

Captain Powers
On the Bridge

In summary, BELKNAP was clearly at fault in the collision. The court martial placed the "legal" blame on Lieutenant Junior Grade Knull whose actions were certainly a direct cause of the collision.

However, it was Captain Shafer who put him in a situation he couldn't handle. Captains of ships are given that title and responsibility and expected to use their experience to avoid putting unqualified officers in positions they can't handle. It is difficult to always be correct in that judgement, for sure. Becoming an OOD is a junior officer's most immediate ambition; charged with the responsibility for the whole ship as he is. Qualification to take on this responsibility must be closely guarded. There is no "test" for this qualification. It's all based on the Captain's judgement and trust, as it should be.

Captain Shafer and Rear Admiral Gureck are both honorable and professional naval officers. We all make mistakes. Captain Shafer's were critical. To his credit, he saved many lives when he gave the order that prevented BELKNAP from crossing KENNEDY's bow and being struck amidships, which would have likely cut the cruiser in half. Captain Gureck had an opportunity to maneuver his ship to avoid collision when KENNEDY and BELKNAP were approaching extremis, but for whatever reason, did not take it. Collision was inevitable.

*****

A series of tragic mistakes resulted in a collision that cost eight Navy men their lives and changed the lives of many others.

It was a proud moment for the ships and men of Destroyer Squadron TWENTY-TWO who were able to lessen the tragedy through the courageous actions of its Sailors. At the same time, it was tragic. The actions of DALE in setting up an emergency trauma center and serving as medical evacuation coordinator saved many lives. The crews of KENNEDY and BELKNAP reacted to the collision and successfully fought hard to save their ships.

It was a night to forget that will never be forgotten.

*****

Epilogue

Excerpts From a Letter From Commodore Schultz to His Wife, 24 November, 1975.

Well your man has had a most demanding and heart rending experience. You read of it in the papers, but you had to see that holocaust to appreciate the absolute horror of BELKNAP burning over ½ of her length and her whole superstructure burned over from colliding with JFK.

My real trial is yet to come as I must testify in the formal investigation of my two good friends Dick (Shafer) and Bill (Gureck) and the details of that tragedy. That starts on the 26th and should be over by the 29th (Bill's change of command day!). What a way to go out!

Anyway, I hope Kathy called you right away before you heard it on press that we were in CVR and safe. (We thought! But let me tell you what happened.) BELKNAP's boiler blew, or one at least, when her stack was closed off from collision and fuel lines probably parted to feed the fire.

Upon collision the JFK also had fire spread to her before getting apart so she was out of it. Admiral Carroll immediately assigned me as On Scene Commander in charge, since he lost communications. The BELKNAP was burning furiously from forward stack to after directors. The whole superstructure less bridge was turned over and burning as I ordered Bob to close to fight the fires and provide assistance to wounded.

As he approached midships I ordered T.C. HART (a frigate) in astern to evacuate many burned Sailors laid out around the fantail. There was no passage from forward to fantail as it was burning hell in between.

I ordered DALE (a cruiser) as the collection point for casualties for small boats from all ships and sent Doc Lieberman (the Squadron Medical Officer) there to set up emergency treatment.

JFK got off two helos, but their ability to work either fantail or foc'sle due to sparks, heat and antennas kept them from being effective. Used them to evacuate the badly burned from DALE to JFK for screening and on routing to Naples and eventually to a burn hospital in Karlsruhe, Germany (where we visited once, remember?)

I sent PHARRIS (a frigate) alongside JFK to fight her fires from alongside, on request from JFK.

Then we got close and the shells (3"/50) and torpedoes were prone to blowing up in the intense heat (at the time, it appeared so, but the torpedoes did not blow up, only the 3"/50 gun ammunition and chaff rockets detonated). Shrapnel like metal chunks fell on CVR as we got closer.

Soon, the whole 3"/50 magazine collapsed on each side and the explosions subsided. We had tried moving in fighting fire from the bow, but could only get limited water over.

Bob was reluctant to get close enough to suit me to do the job needed. I ordered him to get his bow right up close so water volume could bear from over 5 or 6 fire hoses on foc'sle. We moved in to 5 yards off the bow and were doing well but could not get after hoses to bear, so I said to back off, get parallel so we could get enough additional hoses to bear. We did.

Well, once alongside the heavy roll of the sea, as heavy weather set in, was lifting us right into BELKNAP's side on successive heavy rolls. We got all 22 hoses to bear and all six fire pumps put thousands of gallons of water on BELKNAP to drive heat down and suppress fire to about centerline.

The visibility went to zero. We couldn't see the bridge bulwark it was so thick with smoke and steam, I felt us being set in one last big roll and saw BELKNAP just a few feet away at the burned out midships area just in a downward glimpse; Not knowing how we might strike BELKNAP to hole our bow.

Bob was starting to back out at 1/3. I ordered him to back full both engines and just as it took hold the roll hit us right amidships (but RICKETTS failed to strike the BELKNAP). Close!

We still had 18 badly injured on the foc'sle with only our Corpsman from CVR and no way to evacuate with boats from her (BELKNAP'S) high bow. I decided we had to get alongside to get them off and work the remaining ½ of burning midships.

We came about to be bow to bow and Bob made a masterful landing and we put lines over. While holding bow to bow, Sailors passed stretchers across the lifelines as the surge of sea swells set us in. We wiped out all our rubber fenders between the ships after about 1 hour alongside.

I was on same level as Dick Shafer's bridge. He looked dazed yet was functioning and had his fire fighting teams working on both ends of the fire while we covered the middle. He had emergency fire pumps and generators both forward and aft.

Soon he lost the forward one and fire re-flashed up the superstructure burning out CIC (and probably my comfortable cabin!). He had no water forward now except what we gave him from our bridge (on CVR).

We had to stay alongside for over two hours until we got wounded off and got the fire out and had his forward pump restarted (cleared debris from midships to get auxiliary line from aft to forward).

We backed clear about 1:30 AM and evacuated our serious cases to DALE and JFK. W.R. (wardroom) was used as a burn dressing station. Two men were horribly burned over 40% of their body. Went down to encourage them. Such horror still on their faces. No eyelashes or eyebrows. All during being on bridge with Bob, good ole Jerry (Chief Staff Officer) was putting all the details together reporting to me on issues, asking for decisions and plans for sending over more oxygen breathing canisters, burn surgical dressings, water (fresh), food, more pumps, gasoline for them, de-watering devices, hoses, more morphine, stretchers.

Required coordination of reports to Washington, London, back to RADM Carroll. Sent 23 in the 12 hours of the crisis. Chuck (Operations Officer) was superb; calm, cool and collected on the radio circuit. Jim Williams (Ensign) was recorder, "go for", and Willie (Material Officer) was my counsel on fire fighting equipment needed, damage to CVR assessor, coordination with CVR for needs; stability officer to see whether we were saving BELKNAP. She had 5 degrees list. Down to 3' to 4' with water delivered. We put so much water on to cool and put out burning aluminum (superstructure is, you know) and the burning oil (JP-4/5) system; it was an explosive prone condition.

Truly believe the ship would have burned to a hulk if we hadn't gone alongside.

Had BORDELON (a destroyer) go in on opposite side to get burning hot spots that kept flaring up until about 0600 – 8 hours after start. Then the search for missing, identity coordination, names for next of kin and such was a horribly complex problem not solved until 12 hours after the start of of the fire and collision.

We still had a ship to tow (BELKNAP into Augusta Bay for assessment.) Got that going at 0700 using BORDELON. Then sweeps and helicopter coordination of going back to the scene to search. No luck (it was determined later that no one went into the sea)! Lots of debris and a trying day.

Still had reports, coordination of forces, and worry for 36 hours being up. Crumpled for 2 ½ hours, then up until midnight. Slept until 0400 when worry awoke me as the Inspector for Formal Board of Investigation RADM Engen from CINCUSNAVEUR was due and I needed more information researched on who, what, where, how.

Formal Board starts Wednesday through Friday. May be living on board JFK. Appears I'm the senior non-involved person so far to observe the deal. Bob from bridge, me in CIC and on the bridge.

Sweating with testimony and a natural uneasiness of telling it badly for Dick and Bill. Such awesome responsibility and gigantic demand on memory, articulation & physical strength. Just had to share with you my trials and tribulations.

Feel better. Read Bible a bit on issues at hand. I only know that my actions, responses, dedication and courage are all that the Academy built into me – and it paid off in ole Bob and me in our facing up to this horrendous, hazardous task. We're closer than ever before and appreciate each other in a most tried mode – we've been there together!

The land of hard decision, competence, direction and his super crew just being a band of heroes all over the ship – dressing wounds, holding bucking fire hoses for hours, CVR never had a more glorious day for being one fighting unit.

Tell Dave R. (Dave Ricketts), Capt. Bob's theories (and his) paid off handsomely in a crisis situation.

Jose (Commodore's Steward) just brought me a cup of hot tea and lemon. It's nearly 2300 and time to get some rest. Couldn't relax before, may now. Tell 'em (the children) Dad's safe, but for several hours it was a gut wrenching ordeal, my throat was tight and the concern for the Captains of both ships, the missing and dead and the unforgiving nature of mistakes in ship handling plagued my mind.

Most glorious kudo message from RADM Carroll! Also from ADM Bagley in London. More on Bob – we made the decisions, coordinated the whole picture, etc. I can't discount Bob's very brave performance and super ship handling.

Hope you haven't been worried. Hope for mail soon. We go to Naples for follow up on hull dents and scrapes rather than Athens. Be there 29 November to 4 December. Barcelona 9-15 December. No word on Dick Albright's (Commodore Schultz's relief), his transportation, or mine to the States.

End of Commodore Schultz's quoted family letter regarding the on scene aspects of this challenging effort in response to a tragic event on a dark, stormy night.

Commodore Schultz's Footnote: At my award ceremony in the Pentagon where I received the Legion of Merit, Vice Admiral Jim Doyle stated, "Thank God there was a Milt Schultz on scene…" He should have said, "Thank God there was also a Bob Powers."

*****

Excerpts from a letter from Captain Powers to his Mother, Kathryn Carney Powers, and his wife Phyllis Garris Powers, written November 26, 1975 in Augusta Bay, Sicily.

It has been a tragic and exciting several days here for me. Ricketts was directly involved in the rescue of USS BELKNAP after she collided with USS JOHN F. KENNEDY. We were about three miles away when it happened and were the first to arrive to assist Belknap which was engulfed in fire and exploding ordnance.

There was really little choice, as I sent RICKETTS to General Quarters, mustered the fire-fighting teams and went alongside BELKNAP. I took her in right alongside, upwind of the fires and we were able to dump massive amounts of water directly onto the fires that BELKNAP men couldn't reach. After several approaches, we had the fires under control.

At the same time, our boat had been launched and was rescuing survivors from BELKNAP's fantail. The weather was miserable, cold, and windy, with gusting rain and thunderstorms. The seas were big gray rollers that banged RICKETTS up against BELKNAP with ferocity.

We then found that there were injured men on BELKNAP's forecastle that couldn't make it down to a boat from the high cruiser bow. So, I took her in again, put my bow up to hers and we took on 18 injured men, mostly with bad burns and crushed limbs.

While there alongside, BELKNAP lost all power and had no pumps for water to fight fires which were beginning to re-flash throughout the ship. So, we stayed longer, providing fire-fighting water, hoses, pumps, first aid supplies, food and whatever to BELKNAP men who were fighting to save their ship. Finally, fires were again brought under control and RICKETTS backed clear.

We then began the ordeal of transferring the seriously wounded by boat in tossing seas to USS DALE where our Doctor had set up an emergency treatment clinic. From there, they were taken by helo to KENNEDY or on to the hospital at Sigonella. KENNEDY had also caught on fire, but not as seriously and her fires were brought quickly under control.

As morning dawned we began an all day search of the area for any survivors in the water. All told, there have been 4 dead, 2 missing, 27 injured on Belknap and one dead on Kennedy (what I knew at the time).

RICKETTS received a message from the Admiral stating that her actions most likely saved BELKNAP from becoming a total loss. It was a mind-snapping tragedy, but my pride in the performance of my crew knows no bounds!

If the adrenaline ever drains from my system, maybe I'll get some sleep. Do not worry. All is fine. It seems that I'm now held up to be available for the investigation. That shouldn't take long.

*****

Captain Powers' Reflections

The BELKNAP Incident is one of many events in Naval history that teach again and again the high price of laxity, of not doing it the way we know it should be done, even for a moment. This is even truer with the technologies we use and the threats we face today!

Many lives were affected by the BELKNAP Incident. The Navy was also affected. At least two major changes (and probably more) came out of the experience:

1) Aircraft Carrier lighting was changed to make the carrier's perspective easier to see at night.

2) Future ships were designed with steel superstructures (vice aluminum, which melts down too easily). This was a major change since all destroyers after World War II had been designed with steel hulls and aluminum superstructures.

The sea and fate don't give you room for laxness

or error. If you're not always vigilant, always ready, something is going to sneak up and get you. I coined a saying that applies;

Keep your gunpowder dry and seek large targets!
Or,
Always be ready, always seek the best.

*****

A Plan of the Day Note Written by Executive Officer Lieutenant Commander Phil Coady

...for the countless incidents of incredible courage and unselfish nobility displayed by the RICKETTS Crew and the CDS-22 Staff. The spirit of the entire crew was typified by the dozen or so men who manned the hoses on the forecastle during our first two approaches to that burning, erupting ship.
 Despite being engulfed in smoke and steam a mere five feet from the BELKNAP's side, exposed to a rain of debris and shrapnel from the secondary explosions, they stood their ground and poured in the fire fighting water which surely saved that ship. And yet their bravery, as extraordinary as it was, was commonplace onboard the CVR that night and throughout the morning.
 In the two hundred years the Navy and Nation have existed, the historical record has filled with instances where the heroic performance of individually unsung Navy Bluejackets has provided that extra measure of effort required to win the day.
 You CVR Men can now proudly take your place beside them.

*****

After being relieved of command of RICKETTS by Commander Joe King, I attended the National War College in Washington, D.C. While there I attended night school and obtained a Master of Science Degree in International Relations from George Washington University,

I went on to duty in the Pentagon on the staff of the Chief of Naval Operations and worked on bringing the HARPOON and TOMAHAWK missiles to the fleet. These missiles would bring to the Surface Navy a capability long needed; a long range anti-ship capability and the ability to strike targets ashore at very long ranges. Up until the time these weapons were introduced, these missions were the sole realm of carrier based aircraft.

I had an interesting assignment as the Senior Military Assistant to the Chairman of the Defense Science Board. This is a group of senior professionals from academia, business and the retired military who advise the Secretary of Defense. I had the opportunity in that assignment to bring my experience to bear on important decisions at a very high level in the Department of Defense. My education at the U.S. Naval Postgraduate School in Monterey, California (Masters in Electrical Engineering, 1967) stood me in good stead in this assignment.

I worked for an unusual man, Doctor Gene Fubini. He was a recognized defense intellectual who had broad influence on the decisions made by The Secretary of Defense. He also had great influence on my life and career. He taught me how to think through and analyze complex situations.

I continued night school at the Catholic University of America and obtained a Ph.D. in World Politics. These night school sessions were an intellectual relief from bureaucratic days in the Pentagon. Somehow, I also managed to run a Cub Scout Pack and later a Boy Scout Troop.

I went back to sea as "the Commodore", in command of Destroyer Squadron SEVENTEEN based in San Diego, California. There, I had command of nine destroyers and the LAMPS Mark III helicopters embarked.

I had the privilege of assisting in developing anti-submarine warfare tactics for towed array sonars, ships, LAMPS and Navy long range patrol aircraft. My squadron escorted the battleship USS NEW JERSEY (BB-62) to a western Pacific deployment and developed tactics for a battleship task group. My squadron was the escort for the carrier USS CONSTELLATION (CV-64).

After command of Destroyer Squadron SEVENTEEN, I commanded the Surface Warfare Development Group in Little Creek, Virginia. In this command, I developed the Class Tactical Manuals for our newer ships and further developed tactics for missiles and antisubmarine warfare.

I retired from the Naval Service in June, 1987 and started a business in which I developed special warfare tactics for Navy SEALs (Sea, Air Land Commandoes).

Later, I wrote computer models and scenarios for analytical war games which I conducted to determine the warfighting value of various new sensor and weapon systems. In this endeavor, I fully used my education in world politics as well as electrical engineering. I had the privilege of teaching for the U.S. Naval War College for several years, as well as Old Dominion University and the Navy off campus graduate programs.

I had a long and interesting career in the U.S. Navy. There are many things I look back on with pride, and of course, some things I wish I had done differently.

In addition to the performance of the officers and crew of RICKETTS that night in the Ionian Sea, I am proud that my XOs, all of my Department Heads and many of the other officers I worked with remained in the Navy and achieved high rank.

My first XO (Dave) commanded a Landing Ship Tank (LST) and excelled in a special intelligence assignment. He went on to serve in command positions ashore in naval communications.

My second XO (Phil) and the line Department Heads (Steve, Bill and Garry) had destroyer commands and cruiser commands. Ben and Tim were Supply Officers on aircraft carriers, a position to which every Supply Corps Officer aspires.

Phil and Steve were promoted to Rear Admiral.

I had assembled a good group.

*****

BELKNAP was towed back to the U.S. for rebuilding at the Philadelphia Naval Shipyard. She received a new, improved 5-inch gun, updated missile armament, sonar, communications, and radar suites.

BELKNAP was re-commissioned in May 1980.

During the period May, 1985 to March, 1986, she was modified to serve as a Fleet Flagship. She was stationed at Gaeta, Italy with COMMANDER, SIXTH FLEET embarked.

In December 1989, BELKNAP served as the U.S. Flagship at the Malta Summit when President George Bush met with Russian President Mikhail Gorbachev.

On February 15, 1995, BELKNAP was decommissioned and stricken from the Naval Registry.

On September 24, 1998, she was sunk as a target.

*****

Admiral Claude V. Ricketts

Claude Vernon Ricketts was born in Missouri on February 23, 1906, and graduated from the U.S. Naval Academy in 1929. For duty in World War II, he received a Letter of Commendation with ribbon and the Legion of Merit with Combat "V".

Admiral Ricketts commanded the amphibious assault ship USS ALASHAIN (AKA-55). In 1952, he became Head, Amphibious Warfare Branch, Office of the Chief of Naval Operations. He then commanded the heavy cruiser USS SAINT PAUL (CA-73) and served as Commander Destroyer Flotilla FOUR. He was assigned as Director of Strategic Plans, Office of the Chief of Naval Operations.

In 1961, Admiral Ricketts became Commander, Second Fleet and then Vice Chief of Naval Operations. He died while in office.

USS BIDDLE (DDG-5) was renamed USS CLAUDE V. RICKETTS (DDG-5) in honor of Admiral Ricketts. Another ship was later named USS BIDDLE.

THE SHIP
U.S.S. CLAUDE V. RICKETTS (DDG-5)

The ship was laid down as DDG-5 by the New York Shipbuilding Corporation at Camden, New Jersey on 18 May 1959, launched on 4 June 1960 and commissioned as USS BIDDLE on 5 May 1962, at Philadelphia Naval Shipyard. BIDDLE was renamed Claude V. Ricketts on 28 July 1964 in honor of Admiral Claude V. Ricketts, who died on 6 July 1964.

RICKETTS served in the Multilateral Force, manned by a crew made up from Navies of the North Atlantic Treaty Organization (NATO) from June 1964 to the end of 1965. Its crew was drawn from the United States Navy and the Navies of West Germany, Italy, Greece, United Kingdom, Netherlands, and Turkey. RICKETTS served in the Second and Sixth Fleets, operating primarily in the Atlantic Ocean, the Caribbean Sea, the Mediterranean Sea and the Indian Ocean

RICKETTS served as one of the rescue units for USS BELKNAP after her collision with USS JOHN F. KENNEDY on 22 November 1975 - the twelfth anniversary of the assassination of the president so named. The cruiser was ablaze with exploding ammunition and magazines, but the guided-missile destroyer and her crewmen fought and limited damage. Seven crew members aboard BELKNAP and one aboard KENNEDY were killed. For this action RICKETTS received the Navy Unit Commendation.

USS Claude V. Ricketts was decommissioned on 31 October 1989 at Norfolk Naval Station, Norfolk, VA, stricken from the Naval Vessel Register on 1 June 1990. She served honorably and well for 28 years, engaging in operations of the Cold War between the United States and the Soviet Union, including the Cuban Missile Quarantine of 1962.

U.S.S. CLAUDE V. RICKETTS (DDG-5)

Officers
(At the Time of the Rescue Operation)

CDR Robert Carney Powers (Commanding Officer)
LCDR Phillip J. Coady (Executive Officer)
LCDR Steven G. Smith (Engineer Officer)
LT William E. Doud (Operations Officer)
LT Garry Holmstrom (Weapons Officer)
LT Benjamin Welch (Supply Officer)
LTJG Al Kraft (First Lieutenant)
LTJG Greg Geist (Damage Control Assistant)
LTJG Tony Telesmanic (Communications Officer)
LTJG John Woodhouse (Combat Information Officer)
LTJG Al Creasy (Gunnery Assistant)
LTJG Tom Gross (Navigator)
ENS Rich Celotto (Main Propulsion Assistant)
ENS Tim Freihofer (Disbursing Officer)
ENS Mike Nemechek (Electronic Warfare Officer)
ENS Rob McDonough (Fire Control Officer)
ENS John Pic (Anti-submarine Warfare Officer)
ENS Ralph McGee (Boilers Officer)
ENS Rafe Polo (Electrical Officer)
CWO2 Ed Loboda (Electronics Material Officer)

U.S.S. CLAUDE V. RICKETTS (DDG-5)

Chief Petty Officers (At the Time of the Rescue Operation)

Master Chief Machinist's Mate A. Groce
Master Chief Electrician's Mate C. Linn
Master Chief Fire Control Technician (Missiles) J. Austin
Master Chief Gunner's Mate (Missiles) A. Roney
Master Chief Fire Control Technician (Missiles) D. Hooper
Senior Chief Gunner's Mate F. Manning
Senior Chief Boiler Technician J. Brown
Chief Boiler Technician R. Hunt
Chief Machinist's Mate L. McKinney
Chief Electronics Technician R. Barker
Chief Yeoman J. Bowman
Chief Hospital Corpsman J. Coleman
Chief Boatswain's Mate J. Pugh
Chief Fire Control Technician (Guns) L. Bonin
Chief Radioman G. Hale
Chief Storekeeper C. Soltes
Chief Commisaryman O. Greenhouse

Commander, Destroyer Squadron TWENTY-TWO (Embarked)

Officers
(At the Time of the Rescue Operation)

CAPT Milton J. Schultz (Commodore)
LCDR Gerry Lewis (Chief Staff Officer)
LT William. Slover (Material Officer)
LT Thomas Burns (Communications Officer)
LT. Charles Hofer (Operations officer)
LT R. Lieberman (Medical Officer)

Chief Petty Officers
(At the Time of the Rescue Operation)

Chief Radioman S. Haskins
Chief Career Counselor Johnson

Schedule
USS CLAUDE V. RICKETTS (DDG-5)
JANUARY 1975 – JANUARY 1976

27 January: Sea Trials (following overhaul in Norfolk Naval Shipyard)

29-31 January: Naval Ammunition Depot, Earle, New Jersey, load ammunition

1-28 February: Training Exercises, Virginia Capes Operations Area

15 March: Port Everglades, FL, Weapons Acceptance Tests

20-22 March: Andros Island, Bahamas, Sonar Tests

25 March: Roosevelt Roads, Puerto Rico

26-27 March: Missile Test Firings, Roosevelt Roads Operations Area

31 March: Guantanamo Bay, Cuba (GTMO), Refresher Training in local operations areas

19-22 April: Ochos Rios, Jamaica, Port Visit

25 April: Operational Readiness Test

2 May: Departed GTMO

12 May: Norfolk, Virginia

12-30 May: Upkeep and Training in Norfolk

19 July: Departed Norfolk

31 May: Naval Ammunition Depot, Yorktown, Virginia, load ammo

3-6 June: Propulsion Examining Board (PEB) Preparations

10-11 June: Operational Propulsion Plant Examination (OPPE)

29 June: Norfolk, Virginia, Preparations for Overseas Movement (POM)

22 July: Naval Ammunition Depot, Yorktown, Virginia, load ammunition (dependent's cruise)

24 July: Return to Norfolk, Virginia, continue preparations for overseas movement (POM)

29 July: Departed Norfolk, Virginia

8 August: Rota, Spain, Port Visit and CHOP to SIXTH FLEET

12-14 August: National Week Exercise in the Ionian Sea

14 August: Training Anchorage, Augusta Bay, Sicily

15-22 August: Taranto Italy, Port Visit

22-27 August: Task Group Operations with USS JOHN F. KENNEDY (CV-67)

27 August–8 September: Upkeep, Naples, Italy

10-11 September: Souda Bay, Crete, Training Anchorage

11 September: Missile and Gunnery Firing Exercise, Souda Bay Operations Area

12 September: Souda Bay, Crete, Training Anchorage

13-16 September: Kithira, Greece, Training Anchorage

14 September: Visit by Secretary of the Navy at Training Anchorage

16-18 September: Antalya, Turkey, Training Anchorage CHOP to NATO

19 September: NATO Exercise Deep Express, support of amphibious operations in northern Turkey

28-30 September: Kithira, Greece, Training Anchorage

1 October: Visit by Commander Task Force 60

5-10 October: Tyrrhenian Sea, National Week Exercise XIX

10 October: Golfo di Castlemare, Anchorage

14-18 October: Elefsis, Greece (Athens) Port Visit

20 October - 1 November: Tender Availability (for repairs and upkeep), Naples, Italy

13 November: Missile and Gunnery Exercise north of Crete

17-19 November: Augusta Bay, Sicily, Training Anchorage

22 November: COLLISION between USS JOHN F. KENNEDY (CV-67) AND USS BELKNAP (CG-26) in the Ionian Sea west of Sicily. Fire fighting and Rescue Operations

23 November: Search and Rescue Operations

26-28 November: Augusta Bay Sicily, Anchorage

29 November - 4 December: Naples, Italy. COLLISION INVESTIGATION

9-15 December: Barcelona Spain, Port Visit

15-18 November: Anti-Air Warfare Exercises with the Spanish Navy

22 December - 2 January: Palma de Mallorca, Spain, Port Visit

7-12 January: Malaga, Spain, Port Visit

14-16 January: Lisbon, Portugal, Port Visit

27 January: Return to Norfolk, Virginia

Awards
(For the Rescue Operation)

Secretary of the Navy Unit Commendation
(a ribbon worn by the ship, all crew members and embarked squadron personnel serving at the time of the incident)
(The second highest award that can be earned by a ship of the U.S. Navy, the unit equivalent of the Silver Star Medal)

USS CLAUDE V. RICKETTS (DDG-5)

The following medals were awarded:

Legion of Merit (3)

CAPT Milton J. Schultz (CDS-22)
CDR Robert C. Powers (CO)
LCDR Philip J. Coady (XO)

Navy and Marine Corps Medal (for lifesaving) (4)

HMC J. Coleman
LTJG Greg Geist
HT1 R. McClary
BMC J. Pugh

Navy Commendation Medal (37)

LCDR G, Lewis (DESRON 22 CSO)
LCDR S. Smith
LT W. Doud
LT. G. Holmstrom
LT. B. Welch
LTJG A. Kraft
LTJG T. Telesmanic

EMC S. Reburiano

SKC C. Soltes

BM1 F. Adams
EN1 C. Boone
EM1 D. Eaves

OS2 P. Dolan
BM2 N. Price
HT2 R. Williams
HM2 J. Wilson

MM3 G. Bollard
MM3 R. Burns
HT3 G. Giehm
SM3 T. Parsons
HT3 M. Widfeldt

ENFN D. Bowen
TMSN M. Bowling
GMGSN D. Brashier
GMGSN C. Shepherd
HTFN R. Treadway
HTFN D. Ware
SN W. Piluden
SN W. Poindexter
SN A. Priest

MMFA M. Owens
SA W. Jarvina
SA T. Johnson
SA D. Salomon
SA C. Sirls
SA P. Sumera

SR D. Cobb

Navy Achievement Medal (3)

LTJG J. Woodhouse
FTM1 R. Jones

BTFN F. Cushman

COMMANDER, SIXTH FLEET
Letter of Commendation (49)

LT R. Leiberman (DESRON 22 Staff)
LTJG A. Creasy
ENS T. Freihofer
LTJG W. Rowe
CWO2 E. Loboda

ETC R. Barker
MSC O. Greenhouse
FTMC D. Hooper

HT1 C, Bennett
OS1 R. Petty
SK1 D. Sneed

FTM2 M. Aebly
RM2 R. Beaudoin
GMG2 R, Cruse
FTM2 M. Gummo
FTM2 K. Hoy
HT2 R. Lacy
FTM2 R. Morin
FTM2 J. Potter

PN3 D. Bartron
FTM3 F. Carter
HT3 J Cassity
OS3 M. Hodgkins
FTM3 J. King
GMG3 M. Patterson
GMM3 D. Peters
HT3 M. Priestly
FTM3 J. Ruff
SK3 R. Tate
BT3 R. Walmsley
FTM3 W. Zawistowski

SHSN G. Adams
MMFN D. Christiansen
HTFN F. Clore
FTMSN R. Joy
OSSN R. Vincent
SHSA J. Hawkins
BTFA P. Riley
ICFA W. Whitten
RMSA N. Boyle

SN L. Carter
SN R. Furey
FN R. Heckworth
SN R. King
SN F. McGee
FN L. Rivera
SN M. Roberts

FA E. Rice
FA E. Woodford

SR H. Partlow

In Memoriam

The Navy Men who died in the BELKNAP-KENNEDY collision are remembered for their service to their country and as Shipmates;

USS JOHN F. KENNEDY

Petty Officer Second Class (Yeoman) David A. Chivalette, USN

USS BELKNAP

Petty Officer First Class (Machinist Mate) James W. Cass, USN

Petty Officer Second Class (Machinist Mate) Douglas S. Freeman, USN

Petty Officer Second Class (Electrician's Mate) Michael W. Kawola, USN

Petty Officer Second Class (Data Systems Technician) Gordon T. St. Marie, USN

Petty Officer Third Class (Data Systems Technician) Gerald A. Ketcham, Jr., USN

Petty Officer Third Class (Sonarman) Brent W. Larsen, USN

Fireman (Machinist Mate) David A. Messner, USN

Bibliography

1. Chief of Naval Operations Investigation to Inquire into the Circumstances Surrounding the Collision Between USS JOHN F. KENNEDY (CV-67) and USS BELKNAP (CG-26) which occurred on 22 November, 1975, serial 007500878 of September 7, 1976, and related documents

2. Notes and Recollections from Rear Admiral Milton J. Schultz, U.S. Navy (Retired), January 13, 2011

3. Notes and Recollections from Rear Admiral Steven G. Smith, U.S. Navy (Retired), December 26, 2010 to January 21, 2011

4. Notes and Recollections from Captain William H. Doud, U.S. Navy Retired, December 27, 2010 to January 21, 2011

5. Notes and Recollections from Captain Garry Holmstrom, U.S. Navy Retired, December 27, 2010 to January 21, 2011

6. Notes and Recollections from Captain Benjamin Welch U.S. Navy (Supply Corps) Retired, January 19, 2010 to January 21, 2011

7. Notes and Recollections from Captain James Timothy Freihofer, U.S. Navy (Supply Corps) Retired, December 27, 2010 to January 19, 2011

8. Notes and Recollections from Commander Richard Celotto,U.S. Navy Retired, January 12, 2010 to January 10, 2011

9. USS CLAUDE . RICKETTS (DDG-5) Cruise Book 1975-76

10. Margeotes, Michael. History of USS BIDDLE (DDG-5) and USS CLAUDE V. RICKETTS (DDG-5). 2010

11. Ill, Peter, The Belknap-Kennedy Collision; An Encouraging Tragedy, A Senior Thesis submitted to the History Department of Princeton University in partial fulfillment of the requirements for the degree of Bachelor of Arts. April 15, 1981

12. USS CLAUDE V. RICKETTS (DDG-5), Ships Deck Log Sheet, 11/22/75-11/23/75

13. USS CLAUDE V. RICKETTS (DDG-5), Radio Telephone Logs, 11/22/75-11/23/75

14. USS CLAUDE V. RICKETTS (DDG-5), Family Gram, December, 1975

15. The Tin Can Sailor, With Their Backs to the Sea: The USS BELKNAP STORY, July-August 2003

16..USS CLAUDE V. RICKETTS (DDG-5), dead Reckoning Tracer Plots, 22 November 1975

17. Powers, Robert C., The Belknap Rescue, A Chart Presentation, January 16, 2001

18. Time Magazine, " There It Was", December 8, 1977

19. USS Claude V. Ricketts (DDG-5), Ship's History, 1975, OPNAV Report 5750-1

20. USS Claude V. Ricketts (DDG-5), Ship's History, 1976, OPNAV Report 5750-1

*****

Powerful Publisher LLC

publisher@powerfulpublisher.com

www.powerfulpublisher.com